DISCARD

D1172729

SIMPLE ACTS TO CHANGE THE WORLD

500 WAYS TO MAKE A DIFFERENCE

AMY NEUMANN

ADAMS MEDIA

NEW YORK   LONDON   TORONTO   SYDNEY   NEW DELHI

Adams Media
An Imprint of Simon & Schuster, Inc.
57 Littlefield Street
Avon, Massachusetts 02322

Copyright © 2018 by Simon & Schuster, Inc.

All rights reserved, including the right to reproduce this book or portions thereof in any form whatsoever. For information address Adams Media Subsidiary Rights Department, 1230 Avenue of the Americas, New York, NY 10020.

First Adams Media hardcover edition October 2018

ADAMS MEDIA and colophon are trademarks of Simon & Schuster.

For information about special discounts for bulk purchases, please contact Simon & Schuster Special Sales at 1-866-506-1949 or business@simonandschuster.com.

The Simon & Schuster Speakers Bureau can bring authors to your live event. For more information or to book an event contact the Simon & Schuster Speakers Bureau at 1-866-248-3049 or visit our website at www.simonspeakers.com.

Interior design and images by Katrina Machado

Manufactured in the United States of America

10 9 8 7 6 5 4 3 2 1

Library of Congress Cataloging-in-Publication Data has been applied for.

ISBN 978-1-5072-0896-0
ISBN 978-1-5072-0897-7 (ebook)

Many of the designations used by manufacturers and sellers to distinguish their products are claimed as trademarks. Where those designations appear in this book and Simon & Schuster, Inc., was aware of a trademark claim, the designations have been printed with initial capital letters.

To my favorite world changer,
my daughter Isabella Skye.

INTRODUCTION

Today is the perfect day to make a difference and change the world! No matter your interests or experience, there is always a way for you to make a difference—and even the smallest acts go a long way toward creating an impact that matters. In *Simple Acts to Change the World*, you'll find 500 easy ways you can make a difference in the world around you, including:

- Sprucing up the teachers' lounge at your local school
- Sharing your professional skills on a nonprofit pro bono project
- Making comfort kits for kids impacted by natural disasters
- Planting flowers in a common space in your community
- Creating a neighborhood watch
- Becoming a teen peer counselor
- Collecting items for a charity auction

And your impact doesn't end there! As you better the world around you through your acts, you'll also discover that you are bettering yourself along the way. You will learn about others in your community, and make a difference for future generations. Not only that, but in your simple acts, you'll also inspire others to do their own part in making the world a better place. When a neighbor sees you donating an instrument to a nearby school, he may be inspired to give free guitar lessons to local kids. When a friend spots you walking a dog from the community shelter, she may be moved to take in a foster animal. Every time you help increase awareness around important causes and issues, you create new opportunities for more people to learn and take action.

Whether you have just five minutes to spare or have the time for a longer commitment, with *Simple Acts to Change the World*, you'll be ready to step out the door and make that difference.

Donate *sports equipment* to organized sports. Scour your garage for unused equipment your kids have outgrown or you've stopped using. Clubs, churches, or schools can use your equipment to help kids get some fun exercise and learn a new activity. Organized sports teach kids important lessons on responsibility and leadership and are a great way to build community by protecting common spaces for community use, as well as elevating self-esteem among peers.

Help your favorite charity make thank-you calls or write *notes of thanks*. Receiving thanks increases the feeling of doing good for the person who gave. This encourages them to donate again in the future and help further the cause.

Become a *bluebird monitor* (or a monitor of any species of bird competing with invasive species in your community). Set up a bluebird box and follow the nesting of bluebirds and their babies. This will provide valuable information about the local environment, which you can share with organizations like the Bluebird Societies to see more regional, national, or global trends. The information you collect also helps these organizations keep an eye on conservation efforts and understand the health of wildlife on a larger scale.

Offer to take photos at a charity event. Many nonprofits like to share the fun that their guests have at a walkathon, gala, or another event. Photos that are posted to the nonprofit's *social channels* can be shared by the guests later to help more people learn about the nonprofit and encourage them to take part themselves.

Ask your company to work on a *pro bono project*. Pro bono, from the Latin phrase "pro bono publico," or "for the public good," is a focused, longer-term version of volunteering that usually involves professional skills. Pro bono projects can involve accounting, legal services, human resources, marketing, or other skills that can be applied to the needs of nonprofits. Organizations like Catchafire and Taproot list projects available at nonprofits that can use your expertise.

Catalog and sell interesting items for nonprofits using *online auction* sites like *eBay* and *eBid*. Sharing unique items with history can create a buzz for a nonprofit. Because of the large reach these websites have, selling items in this way might also raise more money for the cause than a local garage sale or auction would. And collectors will pay a premium for the uncommon things they collect.

Make trophies for kids. Ask a local nonprofit that works with children if they need any *trophies* created and donated for upcoming events. This unusual donation gives kids something to keep to inspire and encourage them. The trophies can be for things like completing programs, getting good grades, or doing well in friendly competitions.

Drive a *foster pet* on a leg of their trip to their new family. There are dogs and cats all over the world looking for homes, and sometimes the perfect pet is located a town, state, or province away. Owning a pet also has infinite positive effects on people's lives, including reducing stress and loneliness, creating a loving bond, encouraging responsibility, and fostering exercise. As a transport volunteer, you help move pets, often from overcrowded shelters to shelters with more room, or to new homes to make a cuddly love connection.

Watch TED Talks for inspiration. TED's motto is that there are "ideas worth spreading." Watch the most popular talks of all time, or one of the over one hundred other themed playlists such as "Talks by brilliant kids and teens" or "Talks to help you find your purpose," and share your favorite talks with friends, family, or any groups you are a part of. You can also create a group that watches and discusses different talks and how to apply them to your own lives, communities, or the world.

Repair equipment for a nonprofit organization. If you or other people you know have skills in anything related to HVAC, electrical, welding, or other technical trades, those skills are invaluable to organizations with critical equipment that is broken or in need of maintenance.

Help teachers create a debate class. Many organizations offer free debate "tool kits" for teachers to use, and these organizations will appreciate your help with ideas and planning. Debate is a valuable *critical-thinking* skill for kids (and adults). Debate cultivates the ability to see multiple viewpoints on a topic, increases public-speaking confidence, and introduces topics that might not normally be discussed elsewhere.

Make a plot of land in your neighborhood nice. If there's a common space on your street, get your neighbors together and set up a little bench, plant a few flowers, or paint anything that's a bit worse for wear. Simple, small acts to *beautify* one spot will inspire others to freshen up a block or two of their own.

Help organize a "done in a day" project at work. *Done-in-a-day* projects are activities that complete a community project from start to finish in one day of volunteering. Team projects give you and your colleagues some time away from the office to bond and share the great feeling of giving back to the community in visible, tangible ways, in only one day. Some examples of popular projects include playground or shelter painting and cleanup, and landscaping or gardening.

Ask local establishments you frequent or your office manager to switch to motion-detection lightbulbs, use light timers, or invest in programmable thermostats. These small changes can knock *power use*—and bills—down a notch, and are more friendly to your community's environment.

Create a *gratitude list* about your neighborhood for thirty days. Whenever you see something stunning, inspiring, or unique, jot it down. Once you have a nice long list, mention those positive things to people whenever you can. Bonus points if you mention them somewhere like a blog post where others can see them. Foster inspiration and community pride!

Drive a *veteran* to medical, dental, or therapist appointments.

Take a free bias test online. Tests like Project Implicit can help uncover what *subconscious biases* might be hidden to us, and knowing which ones you might have helps open up the world just a little more. These tests are also insightful for large teams, boards of directors, and volunteers who work with the community. You can find Project Implicit at https://implicit.harvard.edu/implicit.

Hold a "sleep out" event to bring awareness to *homelessness*. You can camp overnight in sleeping bags or cardboard boxes in parks and other public spaces. This creates empathy not only within the volunteers who experience what it might feel like to be homeless, but also within everyone who sees or hears about your "sleep out."

Buy *seasonal-themed supplies* in the spring for an organization that works with young kids. The organization can use the supplies for craft time, or to create small gifts to give to the kids to spread cheer in the community.

Adopt a highway as a neighborhood or community organization. The investment by the group is just *picking up litter* along the stretch of highway a couple of times per year (sometimes with modest fees). Your group's name may be on a sign for that year for recognition and awareness within the community as well.

Donate packs of diapers to a local shelter or diaper bank. Diapers are a large monthly cost, which can be a challenge for many families. There are diaper groups that also take donations of money for purchasing diapers in bulk. You can find a *diaper bank* near you through the National Diaper Bank Network at NationalDiaperBankNetwork.org, or internationally at RedCross.org.

Create jars of "*volunteer chores*" for your favorite nonprofit organization. Help the organization come up with a variety of tasks that volunteers can do, then put the "chores" into jars based on ages, skills, or time commitments. You can also put the volunteer chores list online to give more people a chance to help.

Organize a *sock drive*. Invisible People, an organization that documents the stories of homeless people in the United States and Canada, says socks are their most requested item from homeless friends. Buying a few packs when you're at the store is a great start. You can also bring a box to your office or place of worship and ask others to donate. You can give the collection to a local shelter.

Buy *back-to-school supplies* for kids at a local school. There are usually lists online and at local retailers right before the new school year starts with everything students need for different grades. Pick a grade, and buy two, three, or a dozen sets of the items for your neighborhood school.

Support local minority-owned businesses in your area. Supporting *minority-owned businesses* creates additional job opportunities and puts money back into diverse communities, fostering deeper connections between different cultures. A quick online search can usually pull up directories of businesses owned by minorities.

Go "*plogging*": picking up litter while exercising outside. Grab a bag, and pick up stray trash as you go! If you're in a running, walking, or hiking group, ask everybody to join in on the next run, walk, or hike.

Buy an *indoor potted plant* for your next housewarming gift. Indoor plants provide oxygen and beauty and can last a long time (results may vary depending on the gardening skill of your host). This way, your friends will have thoughtful gifts that also help the environment.

Introduce yourself to people you see locally all the time. A quick "Hi! I'm Jane. Since we see each other all the time, what's your name?" will do the trick. You'll feel more like neighbors and will encourage other people to do the same, making the community friendlier.

Team up with friends or an organization to build a *Little Free Library*. These creative book exchange libraries are set up outside in the community to encourage reading, as well as sharing. Once it's built, you can collect books once or twice a year to rejuvenate the library.

Donate unsold items from a yard sale, especially furniture. Thrift stores and local *furniture banks* will give unsold items new homes. Furniture banks give furnishings to displaced people who need them.

Create a short *how-to video* about something you are uniquely skilled at doing, and share it online. You can help a lot of people learn that skill!

Help your favorite charity sign up for *Amazon Smile* and share it with their supporters. This free program donates half a percent of all eligible purchases back to a cause with no strings attached.

Ask friends to donate *dress clothes* like business suits to organizations like Dress for Success, or a local shelter. Suitable attire for interviews can be expensive but can make all the difference in creating a good first impression and securing a job. If you haven't worn that one suit in a while, set it free to help land someone a new job!

Create a *secret band of do-gooders*. Pick something fun and compassionate to do each week. For example, one week you can all hide a few dollars in books at the local library; the next week you can tip double your normal amount at restaurants, or write and mail handwritten thank-you cards to three people you appreciate.

Help someone who wants to start a *small business* take the first steps. Being an entrepreneur holds numerous rewards, not only for the business owner, but also for the community. It creates jobs, provides tax revenue for the locality, encourages local community involvement, promotes innovation, and provides a sense of pride and accomplishment for the owner and his or her family. There are infinite resources online to help get started, or to find a local organization that can assist directly.

Upcycle from thrift stores. This saves both money and resources, and keeps items out of landfills. Those chairs or lamps that look vintage in a less-than-desirable way can be turned into showstoppers with some spray paint! Take items to a local organization and hold a class on upcycling, then donate the glorious new masterpieces to a nonprofit that needs them!

Know an overwhelmed parent this *holiday season*? Take a load off their shoulders—and create smiles— by bringing their child to see Santa at a local mall or event. Be sure to take pictures!

Take public transportation when you travel. Taking taxis can remove some of the most interesting sights, sounds, and experiences from a journey. On top of supporting local jobs and reducing pollution and traffic impact, using *public transportation* allows you the freedom and flexibility to connect to more people in that community and gain a greater appreciation for the place you're visiting!

Do some background research on a company. *Sustainable companies* focus on important areas like environmental impact, social issues, and the creation of high-quality workplaces. These companies also tend to perform better financially in the long term, positively affecting the economy. If you find a company that stands out, give them good reviews online and share their information with friends, family, and coworkers.

Give a *business loan* to someone. Small businesses can have big positive effects in communities by providing local employment opportunities, keeping money in the local community, and promoting local investment in resources related to businesses, so even small investments can go a long way.

Help people find the *final resting places* of their loved ones. BillionGraves and Find a Grave are crowdsourced international apps that match details of headstones to inquiries about where loved ones are buried. Volunteers help complete the databases, often with photos and coordinates of headstones.

Get a group together to be a *route cheering team* at a walkathon or other charity race. Some simple (or funny) poster board signs, festive cheering and clapping, and maybe a cowbell or two are all you need to encourage someone to press on just a bit more!

Create *entertainment bags for kids* in the hospital. Inexpensive items like coloring books and crayons, a small chalkboard and chalk, a small cookie sheet and magnets, or other age-appropriate and safe items can keep kids happy and focused on positivity.

Volunteer to *babysit* kids while their parents attend classes or go back to school. Babysitting cooperatives are another option for parents who need babysitters, providing a "babysitter swapping" option. Visit SittingAround.com for more information.

Organize items at a secondhand store. If you have some organizing skills and an eye for presentation, you might be the perfect person to help a local charitable *thrift shop* catalog, organize, and display items for sale so the store can sell more treasures. Then, they can use those extra dollars to fund their core mission.

Become a *coach* for an unusual game, like bubble soccer, that simply is designed to be fun. Or join a team that is already established. Community sports groups help people bond and learn more about their neighbors.

Donate *bus passes* to a local shelter to help residents get around town.

Become a *citizen scientist*. Local organizations need your help monitoring things like water quality. Your local department of natural resources may need volunteers to take samples. Having up-to-date information on water quality and other environmental elements can help keep the community safe, and identify any troubling trends in time to make corrections.

Teach adults how to *read*. Not being able to read creates a whole host of barriers for adults, from navigating transportation and healthcare to employment issues. Teaching people to read can drastically change their lives and the lives of their loved ones.

Collect items for a *charity auction*. Ask local merchants for gift cards or items for gift baskets. This gives local merchants positive recognition at the auction, and the proceeds from the auction support the charity's efforts in the community.

Help people write compelling resumes. If you have some skills in the business arena, *resume writing* is a great way to give back. You can even offer to teach a class on the topic. A strong resume can be the key that opens the door to a new job!

Visit and chat with *hospice patients*. You can learn from stories that the patients share about their lives, and give them comfort and a kind smile.

Keep *first aid kits* in your car, office, and home. You can buy them or make them yourself. This way, if someone around you needs a quick fix, you have basic items to provide.

Learn CPR. Even if you're unlikely to ever need to use it, knowing cardiopulmonary resuscitation in the event that someone stops breathing because of heart attack, stroke, or another medical emergency might save a person's life. The Red Cross offers CPR classes and certification. This is an excellent skill for babysitters to learn as well!

Carry jumper cables in your vehicle, and learn how to use them. The next time someone needs a jump, you can save their day!

Give tours at your favorite nature center. Once you receive some basic volunteer training, you can share your passion for the natural world with others, introducing them to new ideas and beauty that they can appreciate whenever they go hiking or visit parks.

Get a group together to write a few simple words of inspiration or appreciation on small note cards, and leave them in appropriate public areas (without littering) as an *uplifting surprise* for people to find. This will spread some unexpected joy in your community.

Drop off *coffee and treats* for the staff at your favorite small nonprofit. Goodies can help fuel the good they do all day long!

Help someone prepare their taxes. Many organizations provide free *tax services* to individuals who earn under a certain income level, so if you are an accountant, you can do it formally. You can also teach a group at a senior center or your local library. Or if you're just good at taxes and don't mind doing them, show friends or relatives the basics, or how to use tax software.

Start or join a running, walking, or hiking club in your community. In addition to being good *exercise*, it will give you time to chat with new people on a regular basis. You can learn more about them and about the places you run, walk, or hike. Connecting with neighbors and exploring local areas creates a sense of community and an appreciation for one another, as well as the places you share!

Say *"thank you"* to ten people today.

Study another religion. Ask people you know from other religions to share their thoughts, and discuss what you learn with people you know. Learning about global religions can bring new insight into economic, military, cultural, and other areas of world policy, and help *foster peace*.

Make the office a more *eco-friendly* place. Buy some real cups, mugs, plates, or silverware for your office kitchen. Buy a water-purifying faucet device. It is estimated that skipping bottled water saves the average person more than $250 per year, and your office mates can enjoy some of those savings too!

Take a *time-management* class so you can fit more things you've been wanting to do to change the world into your schedule. You could make more time for things that benefit you and others around you— from teaching a skill or volunteering at a nonprofit to starting an exercise club.

Donate flowers and shrubs to organizations that can use a little exterior sprucing. You can also offer to help plant them. Adding *curb appeal* to common areas encourages the people who staff those organizations, as well as people who visit.

Practice being the first person to *break the ice* in group activities, such as when volunteering. It can be uncomfortable at first when strangers gather together, and having someone start the conversation can put the whole group at ease. A group who is comfortable will get more work done, creating a bigger impact!

Repaint a room at a favorite organization. This can be an organized large group project, or you can do it with just a couple of people. Paint refreshes a space and makes it feel new, bringing invigorating and *positive energy* to the organization!

Create a "dinner tree" or meal train. Coordinate with a group of friends to deliver *cooked meals* each day for a week or two (or longer). The meals can be for anyone who could use a hand with dinner—maybe the family of someone who just had a baby, is ill, or recently had surgery.

Offer to answer phone calls or be a *greeter* in the lobby of an organization. You'll get a feel for what types of services they provide and have a chance to meet and help the people they serve!

Find *volunteer opportunities* that match your interests and skills with websites like VolunteerMatch.org, *HandsOn Network*, or Idealist.org.

Get kids in on the fun of *giving*. Next time you're at a dollar store with kids, ask them to help pick out some items for other kids, or for people without homes. It's a fun activity for kids, and they will enjoy thinking about people using the items they select and give!

Travel abroad (almost free) and help your *global neighbors*. Wherever you live, there are opportunities to explore another country and learn new skills while assisting others. Many organizations offer things like free room and board for your help, as well as the chance to expand your horizons.

Start a *social media* group or page for something you care about in your hometown such as parks, neighborhood events, recreation options, bird-watching—you name it. If you're passionate, you can encourage friends and neighbors to get passionate too! Let them join in creating or updating the page with photos and personal comments. Together you will create more awareness for the things that make your community great, or that need a little more tender love and care.

Plant a *butterfly garden*. Attracting beautiful butterflies can be done with nectar plants and other butterfly-friendly options found at your local garden center. These colorful creatures help pollinate and are important to local ecosystems. Healthy local ecosystems also help to create healthy regions—even small contributions to a healthy environment add up!

Speak up when someone makes an offensive remark or joke.

Teach people how to swim. Swimming is a playful, fun exercise—and is also potentially lifesaving. Donate to *swim lessons* at a swim school or YMCA, or teach some basics yourself. Any age is a good age to learn to swim, adults included!

Give up your seat on a train or bus for anyone who looks tired, who looks stressed, or who may have trouble standing for a long period of time.

Go *electronic*. If you're getting things in the mail that you don't read, there are services to remove yourself from most mailing lists in bulk. This is good for the environment, and your mailbox. It can also help your favorite charity save money. Ask them to limit mailings to only one or two key things you like to open, and continue to support them with online donations instead of paper checks. Suggest that they list electronic ways to connect with them in the mail that they send, so other people can elect to save them money and paper as well.

Register as an *organ donor*. This simple act could save multiple lives!

When you discover a new local gem, like a cute mom-and-pop store or restaurant, be sure to share it with your friends and family. Take a walk on Main Street. Take in the history and charm of your town center and other parts of your city. Then, share any fun discovery with an online review, a shout-out in a *Facebook* post, or an *Instagram* picture with the location tagged and a nice comment or observation so others can see. *Promote doing business locally* and support your neighbors!

Refer job-hunting friends and family to cause-related websites with nonprofit job listings like *The Chronicle of Philanthropy, The Nonprofit Times, Foundation Center, Encore,* or *Commongood Careers.* These sites list *career opportunities* at nonprofits for those who want to make a difference every day.

Set up recurring *online donations*. If you usually send charities a yearly check, consider going to their website and making smaller, automatic monthly donations instead. Charities appreciate knowing how much revenue they can plan for, and it saves them time as well as money to not process paper checks or manually enter information into databases. Encourage others to do the same.

Help your kids or coworkers get into the giving spirit with a penny war. Each group has a container for collecting pennies, which adds money to their team's goal. Other coins or dollars dropped in the container subtract value. So, by making donations other than pennies into your competition's penny container, you win the war, while your donation "wins" for those it helps. This friendly competition promotes bigger donations across the groups, so more money can go to the chosen cause!

Walk a shelter dog. Many animal shelters can use dog walkers. Walking dogs helps them burn off energy, mix with other dogs, and feel loved. There are also opportunities to help process adoptions, socialize animals, or tidy up the shelter. Show some puppy love!

Write a *hotline number* for human trafficking on the inner tags of clothes before you donate them to shelters. Many trafficking victims end up in shelters, so this number could be the help they need!

Take a *cooking class*, then share what you learn. Freshly prepared food can save time, money, and resources, and supports your community when locally grown items are included. Cooking classes (or online videos) can also give you new ideas for vegetarian, vegan, gluten-free, nondairy, and regional or cultural meals that help you learn about your area and help more neighbors feel included in meals.

Collect a neighbor's mail for them when they are away. Not only is this a nice act, but it also prevents the house from being a target for burglars. Burglars often look for mail piling up in a mailbox or on a front porch, as it is a sign that no one is home.

Know Morse code for SOS. In Morse code, an *SOS* distress/emergency signal is three dots, three dashes, three dots—or three short taps, three long taps, three short taps. It can also be done with a whistle, mirrors reflecting light, stones on a beach, smoke signals, or light from a flashlight. Share this code with everyone you know: it can bring help in a dire situation, or even help rescue a group of people!

Give children smiles. Operation Smile and similar organizations fix *cleft palates*. In many countries, children with cleft palates are ridiculed and shunned. A simple operation that takes less than an hour can fix a cleft palate and change a child's life. The more donations received, the more children can receive a life-altering surgery!

Offer up your social media skills. Social media can be a great way for nonprofits to keep in touch with supporters. If you're good at spotting interesting news and information to share, you can help curate social media updates. If you love a specific platform or know a lot about social media *marketing*, you can also offer to provide training.

Make a pillowcase dress for a girl in Africa. These *simple-to-make dresses* become prized possessions of little girls in need, and foster conversations about clean water, education, and community. Visit LittleDressesforAfrica.org for directions and details.

Hold a debate within a group you are part of. Take one side, then take the opposite view. Do some research beforehand and present your case. This may highlight *common ground* on the issue on a larger scale, and encourage people to explore different ideas with an open mind.

Ask your kids to save *ten percent* of their earnings or allowance and give it to a charity of their choice. Saving promotes long-term thinking and patience, and giving helps kids to become better world citizens.

Change a young girl's life. Speak Up for the Poor allows you to support a girl *living in poverty* in Bangladesh. Many of these girls are forced into child marriages to provide an income for their families. Your donation will help prevent a girl from becoming a child bride, and will also enable her to go to (or stay in) school.

Help a friend, family member, or neighbor *pack up* or move their things to a new apartment, house, or dorm.

Help teens at local schools or community centers open retirement accounts. Even if your country will have a government-sponsored *retirement program* of some kind, saving often and early provides additional security. And in the future, adults with more savings will have more money to contribute to projects that make the world a better place!

Grow your own herbs all year and share your harvest with friends, family, coworkers, and neighbors. Many herbs, including mint, rosemary, and parsley, do well indoors. Fresh herbs smell wonderful, look pretty in pots, taste delicious, and save money. Take a planted pot of herbs to work, for the office kitchen or a windowsill. Extra herbs can be dried or frozen in olive oil for use in cooking later, so you can give them to people at any time.

Read a *survival guide* and memorize a few key things. In disaster situations, knowing how to light a fire, navigate directions, find or desalinize water, or keep warm could save you, your family, your neighbors, or your coworkers!

Gather a group and break a *crazy world record* for a cause. A popular way to break a world record is by running while doing something else, like dressing up in costume, juggling something, or even Hula-Hooping. The media attention can help your cause get a lot more visibility. What world record could you break?

Take five minutes to *be thankful* each day. List the things you are grateful for, and feel deep appreciation for them. To really share the feeling of gratitude, get some beautiful note cards and write one to each person in your life that you appreciate. Drop the cards in the mail.

Call someone. Sure, it might go to voice mail—but when the recipient hears it, they will appreciate your hello. You never know who might be in need of a reminder that they are loved.

Share laughs. Take friends to a comedy club. Watch a funny movie as a group event. Laughing releases endorphins that make people happy, and even reduce pain! Your part in making someone *laugh* can make their day, week, or even year.

Salt the stairs or walkways of a community space or apartment building during the colder months.

Start a *book club* locally that features nonprofit, social justice topics. Stimulate creative conversations that benefit the greater good!

Spark some interesting conversations with friends, family, and colleagues by reading the news as presented in other countries and discussing what you hear. Is the *point of view* the same as in your home country? What can you learn from the open discussion? Proactively challenging your preconceptions can broaden your view of the world and create a better understanding of other people and cultures!

Help people shift their energy to *positivity*. Any situation can be perceived through many different lenses, including negative or positive. Focusing on seeing the positive in a situation or conversation can help shift someone's mood, or change the tone of a group. You can start by not contributing to negativity in conversations.

Brew a pot of coffee for the office. In offices, individual-cup brewers can be good for variety, but if everyone just wants a regular cup of coffee, try a traditional coffeepot system. Making one big pot saves everyone time. This simple act of *thoughtfulness* will also make your coworkers smile and give them a moment to pause, relax, and recharge—and perhaps inspire them to do a little something nice for others.

Listen carefully. If someone talks to you about abuse, harassment, a desire to hurt themselves or others, or some other troubling problem, *listen without judgment*. Offer help, like giving them a suicide prevention hotline number (a global list can be found at Suicide.org) or attending a therapy session with them. If needed, report the problem. Many people in need of assistance don't know what to do or who to tell, and your compassion can help them proceed. Even a story about "a friend" in need could be a cry for help.

Grow a mustache (or move, by setting distance goals for running, cycling, or swimming and raising funds for each goal reached) in November's *Movember* movement. The global organization Movember Foundation (found at Movember.com) started with a few fellows growing mustaches for a good cause. Now, more than five million men (and women) participate in different events to raise money for testicular and prostate cancer research each year. Let the mustachery move you to help others!

Fix an old bike for someone. Or donate one to a local bike shop that fixes up old bikes and donates them. Websites like *craigslist* and *The Freecycle Network* often have *free bikes* listed that people are giving away. Bikes provide a way to get around quickly and are a healthy choice for transportation. Whether it's the only way to get somewhere or a more environmentally friendly way to get somewhere, having a working bike is a good thing.

Bring a *meat-free* dish to your next potluck. Meat is extremely resource-intensive to produce, and creates land and pollution issues. Try making and sharing a meat-free dish with unusual meat substitutes like jackfruit or walnuts—your recipes just may inspire others to go meat-free once in a while!

Prevent vampires at work. Vampire electrical use happens with all sorts of devices; even when they're turned off, devices still suck electricity from the outlet they are attached to. Buy power strips/surge protectors with an on-off switch. Keep them "off" unless you're using a device, and turn them all off on the weekends. Even a few office devices plugged in and switched off or into "standby" mode can save large amounts of money in *energy costs* annually. Ask your HR department to donate the savings to a good cause!

Get a group of friends to be *vegetarian* for a month. Make it a contest! Over the course of a year, vegetarian eating can save a good deal of money, and it is also beneficial to your health and the environment.

Cut people a break. The next time you have to wait a long time in a line, or on the phone with customer service, imagine you're the person helping you. Did someone not come in to their shift on time? Is everyone venting at them today? How would you feel if it was your job to handle people's problems all day? Take a deep breath and *ask how their day is going*: it can immediately reduce their stress and reset their mood.

Walk or drive around your neighborhood and write down any streets, signs, or fences in public spaces that need *repair*. Write, call, or email your local government officials and let them know what needs fixing.

Ask people about their tattoos. They usually have an intriguing story. Every story expands your worldview, and striking up conversations with a wide variety of people can *uncover life experiences*, viewpoints, artistic insights, and other things that foster appreciation and personal growth. And you might make that person's day by admiring their art!

Bake some cookies to give your postal worker, or have a hot cup of coffee ready "to go" for your garbage collector early one morning.

Try something new—especially with others—even if it feels awkward. Trying something new is usually uncomfortable. It's also the only way to grow. Take some friends to a place they've mentioned wanting to go, or take kids to *explore* new parks or museums, and ask them what they learned afterward. New things expand the world for people who are adventurous and curious. And expanding the world creates positive change!

Give a dollar a day. Several nonprofits let you give a dollar a day to help provide simple but critical needs like bus tickets, cell phones, or groceries for people facing illness or living in poverty. You could also save a dollar each day in a jar and donate your stash of dollars to one or several causes each month.

Start discussions or a local group to really talk about racism. Many countries have a history of systemic racism and discrimination. Knowing the history of your country and how it impacts current citizens can go a long way toward righting any wrongs. Brainstorm ways to prevent *unintentional prejudice*, create awareness about stereotypes, or think of other actions you and your neighbors can take to help stem racism. Make sure history never repeats itself!

Host a *pet costume parade* where the pet "parents" wear matching costumes. It's not just a great Halloween idea: it could be quite the media event too! Who doesn't love cute pets in costumes? And what is funnier than their pet parent in the same costume? Get the participants to request donations from friends and family for a cause, such as supporting a local animal shelter, and every tail will be wagging!

Attend a seminar or workshop on something important to your community. For example, learn how to facilitate *grassroots efforts* or create a budget for a start-up nonprofit. Share what you learn with other like-minded people who want to create change with you!

Invite an *interesting speaker* to your town. It can be someone famous, or an expert who can help in a niche way by sharing something topical with your city, like how a larger city is handling a similar economic or social challenge. This generates interest and gathers people together in support of a common cause.

Build a home—globally. Habitat for Humanity allows you to share your skills and *travel the world* at the same time, creating a safe place for a family in need.

March to support a cause. You might know the right cause for you when you hear about it; if it moves you, take part in a march in whatever way feels best. Being part of a group effort brings more attention to an issue!

Ask a local restaurant to switch to *hand dryers* instead of paper towels, donate daily leftover fresh food, use trans fat–free oils, or eliminate plastic drinking straws. If you notice something that could be a positive change, mention it!

Collect old *cell phones* to give to organizations that support victims of domestic violence, or other people in dangerous or emergency situations. A flip phone might not be the latest trend, but for someone without a way to communicate, especially in times of emergency, it literally could be a lifesaver!

Donate a few trees to local organizations. Buy (or find a nursery to donate) real trees or saplings and help plant them on their grounds. In addition to making spaces green, and providing oxygen and shade, trees can create privacy and *a connection to nature.*

During gift-giving holidays, go to a local retailer who offers *layaway plans*, and pay off one or two items as a secret surprise. People usually put items on layaway when they don't have the money to spend all at once. Paying a layaway item off is a financial relief to someone who is trying to give the perfect gift to someone special.

Get people together to write personal cards of appreciation for *military troops* stationed overseas. A simple, handwritten card or note (and a few goodies like nonperishable snacks, books, and toiletries like bodywash or lip balm) lends a feeling of home.

Collect or save *magazines* to donate to healthcare or dental offices in lower-income areas for their waiting rooms.

Know and share the risks associated with opioid prescriptions, and ask people you care about to consider alternative medicine, yoga, meditation, or *non-opioid pain relievers* instead. There is a high risk of addiction with opioids that many people do not realize, so if another option could work well, avoiding opioids could prevent a potentially devastating problem altogether. Warn friends about not letting their kids use opioids for things like simple dental procedures or sprains if alternatives will suffice.

Help others understand which local government representatives in your town are working to support goals you endorse. Representatives, like school board members, council members, mayors, and county officials, not mentioned as often in the news can have a big impact on *local policies* that affect you and your neighbors. Talk about the issues these officials support with your friends. Talk to those local representatives, ask them questions to more fully understand their views, and let them know your ideas and opinions. If the representatives are doing a solid job, let people know and help rally support for them!

Take an extra moment to hold open the door for someone, or run ahead of someone carrying a heavy load and *grab the door* for them.

Create a unique *walking map* of a favorite local area. It could be a park, museum or another educational site, neighborhood, or business district. Highlight a few interesting or unusual things to look for, and note some history. Give the finished map to the park district, chamber of commerce, tourism office, or another organization that will share this unique experience with visitors. A charming and unexpected perspective that helps visitors see and feel how lovely your city is helps those visitors to remember their fun experience and encourage others to visit your city.

Create a group of "*first friends*" (the first person someone new is introduced to, who befriends, guides, and helps them) to support people who are new to your town, your school, or your office. These "first friends" can show the new people around and provide some useful websites, contacts, or resources to help them navigate the area.

Help *translate documents*. Do you or someone you know speak a second language? Many organizations need help translating their most popular documents, like applications for services, instruction manuals, or resource lists, into several other languages spoken by the people they serve.

Turn a personal hobby into a *bigger project*. Love knitting? Get a group together to combine small projects into something big. "Yarn bombing" is when street art is created by fitting colorful knits to objects in the area to brighten things up and give passersby a smile.

Uncover all the places that people can get *free Wi-Fi* or free access to computers in your area. Make a printed and digital list and distribute it to organizations that serve people who may not have Internet access at home.

Check your vocabulary and give a bit of food at the same time. If you have a minute while waiting somewhere like the grocery checkout line, play a fun quiz on FreeRice.com. For each correct answer, the website donates ten grains of rice to help *end world hunger*. Let other people know about it so they can give too!

Have some simple crafting skills? Teach others at a senior center or an elementary school. If the craft is one people will want to buy, help organize a fundraiser to sell the crafts that were made, and donate the proceeds to something that the senior center or classroom needs!

Help your community feel the music. Did your kids give up the clarinet or trombone after high school? Do you have some latent musical skills? Donate old instruments, or play them somewhere community members can enjoy the music. If you're able, teach some music classes. Even casual classes for guitar or piano can help kids feel the joy of music while also learning rhythm, counting, and good practice skills!

Help at a water station during a fun run, walkathon, marathon, or another athletic course event. Cheer people on as they go by, and make sure they stay hydrated!

Make a *mini-event*. Is there something going on nationally, maybe in a city far away, that you're interested in? Try setting up a smaller version of the event locally. Hold a march with a few dozen or hundred people on the same day and at the same time that the larger national march event happens, for example.

Get up and do something when sitting or hanging around is usually the norm. The time after big holiday meals or events together with friends or family can be spent many ways. Rather than watching TV, diving into individual digital devices, or napping, consider visiting a homeless shelter, domestic violence shelter, or senior center, or other places where people might like visitors to bring them some *yummy treats*.

Be a regular volunteer, and *recruit others* to do the same. Many organizations need volunteers all the time, and it's hard for them to figure out who is available and when. If your schedule allows, volunteer consistently on specific days at specific times that work for the organization. Try to bring new people with you when you can.

Try *ten minutes* this afternoon. As Lao-Tzu said, "A journey of a thousand miles begins with one step." Don't let the size of a challenge keep you from helping. You don't have to solve world hunger: you can help feed five more people in your hometown this month. If you have a big activism goal, start by doing something for ten minutes today. It all adds up, and it all makes a difference!

Save an animal. Pets are good for the soul and make great companions. Sometimes, circumstances force people to give up their pets, even when they don't want to. Those cats, dogs, and other furry, finned, feathered, or scaled friends can end up in animal shelters. One (or several) of those shelter pets could be an incredible new companion for you. If you have friends or family looking to adopt pets, suggest the option of *shelter pets*.

Dispose of prescription drugs safely to prevent misuse. Opioids and other drugs are a serious problem in many parts of the world. Drugs should not be flushed down toilets or drains: if they are, they enter the water supply. Unused prescription drugs should be dropped off at safe *local disposal sites*, such as police stations, or combined uncrushed with dirt, coffee grounds, or kitty litter in a bag and disposed of in the trash. Properly removing unused medications means no one can take or distribute those drugs without your knowledge.

Be an *after-school helper*. Kids do lots of things after school: sports, clubs, studying, latchkey (childcare) programs. How can you help? Ask a local school or after-school organization what they need, whether it's people to work with the kids, money, or donated items for the programs.

Make some homemade *natural pet treats* for pets in your neighborhood (or even for your own best friend). A quick search online will reveal a wide array of healthy, natural, and adorable treat recipes pets will love.

Be a *teen peer counselor*. Teens want to talk about their problems to other teens who understand them. If you are a teen, consider volunteering in programs that can train you to listen for and help solve problems for other teens. If you are older, reach out to teens you know to encourage them to become a peer counselor.

Give a few *new toys*. Kids facing troubles such as homelessness, violence, or poverty don't always get to celebrate birthdays or other holidays. Pick up a few new toys and donate them to organizations that serve kids. Many organizations also take gently used toys and books.

Think *globally*. Anything you might want to do locally, you can probably do globally. Kids in Africa need school supplies just like your local kids do. Kids in Asia need medications just like your local kids do. If you're passionate about something, consider helping people outside your own country in addition to those inside your country.

Capture someone's history. StoryCorps.org has a free app you can use to *record an interview* with someone, and you can even add it to the website database (with their permission) for others to enjoy. Highlight local people, or people special to you. You can also find a good home for the stories in places like mainstream publications, blogs, or social media pages. Sharing the wisdom and stories of individuals contributes to the wisdom of larger groups.

Ask your veterinarian if they need any help, from providing supplies to *creating awareness* around key animal safety and health issues such as spaying and neutering. They might even need things that are simple to provide and often used, such as zip-top bags, dish soap, towels, cotton balls and Q-tips, latex gloves, or treats, if they don't have direct animal needs right now. They also may refer you to shelters or other organizations that need help if they don't.

Help kids and adults with functional needs make their voices heard. Not everyone who has functional needs such as physical or developmental challenges is heard during the normal governmental process. This is also true in healthcare, education, housing, employment, and other areas. Be an *advocate* for people who may not be as able to speak up for themselves.

Help foster peace. The goal of the One Billion Acts of Peace campaign is to inspire *one billion acts of peace* by 2020. You can record an act to contribute to their website, BillionActs.org.

Donate to organizations like Living Paintings, an organization that provides "*touch to see*" tactile books for partially sighted and blind people of all ages. This allows more people to better experience and enjoy reading and art.

Donate an Embrace *baby warmer*. EmbraceGlobal.org provides lifesaving warmers for newborn babies to help prevent deaths caused by hypothermia. The warmers are reusable, so you can help save many babies!

Create the story you'd like to hear. If you work with an organization that seems like they could improve their *outreach efforts*—maybe their message seems a bit unclear, or it's being put in a place not many people see—share your thoughts with them. Nobody wants to waste time, energy, or money. If you think they could do better by trying something new, let them know.

Adopt a *zoo animal*. They're like pets, but easier to maintain (for you). Donating to your local zoo helps people from all socioeconomic backgrounds experience, enjoy, and love the animals that make the world diverse!

Throw a *neighborhood festival*. Find something unique about your neighborhood, and celebrate it. Ask your neighbors to get involved with planning the food, entertainment, and activities. You can also pick a cause to help and let local media know about your endeavor. Share the good of your neighborhood!

Share science by taking a group of kids to a science center.

Get a group to *sponsor a series of meals* at a Ronald McDonald House. These international houses for the families of ill children are located close to hospitals, and meals provided by volunteers help the families feel more at home in times of crisis.

Find out if abandoned homes in your area can be purchased by land trusts or other neighborhood organizations. They could be refurbished and sold, or maybe even become museums for local history or study facilities. Help to facilitate a project like this and *turn a lump of coal into a diamond*!

Make it a Month. Choose a project like picking up trash and make a "Picking Up Trash Month." It sounds official, and you can make it a *Facebook* group! Provide "official" acknowledgments like listing everyone who participates on your online page.

Find out what teens are up to. Form a high school *"real-time info" group*. Invite teens to tell you what problems they are hearing about right now. The feedback might not be entirely representative, but it will be insightful. Discover what problems are worth addressing.

Thank the night shift. Doctors, nurses, and other medical staff work hard for us twenty-four hours a day. Bring some thoughtful items like edible treats and flowers to your *local hospital staff*.

Are you a student? See if you can get a spot on your local *community council*. Your viewpoint is important. Have friends join you at meetings to learn and share their ideas.

Gather together an *impromptu choir*. Singing is one of the oldest art forms, known to bring communities together. Find some kindred spirits with a passion for singing and perform at local venues, senior centers, or other places where people would love to hear an uplifting live performance!

Write to the *editorial board* of your local news organizations. It might sound old-fashioned, but editorial boards still have a lot of power. Typically, editorial boards are on newspapers, as well as their digital editions. They are the people who decide the tone and direction taken by the media on any issue in your town. They are influential. And they are keen on understanding all of the dynamics of important issues happening in their hometown. Help them by providing important data, contact people, and facts about an issue.

Coordinate a contact campaign for anything you strongly support. Use email, *Twitter*, phone calls, blogs, or whatever you feel your government official pays attention to in order to help your viewpoint *be heard*.

Donate to organizations that provide free *wellness checkups*. Staying healthy reduces the need for expensive healthcare later. Let other people know about these organizations.

Join your *school board*. If you have a child in a school district, it's especially important to know what that district is doing. And if you're on the school board, you can potentially impact what that district is doing to help the kids there.

Get kids involved in community impact. Pass out flyers for your favorite nonprofit with them. Let your kids feel the weight and importance of doing something and recognizing why it matters!

Write an article for a blog, local newspaper, school paper, *Facebook*, or *LinkedIn*. Choose a topic you are passionate about sharing with others, such as education, community activities, children's issues, animals, or disability rights. *Voices matter.* Share yours. Ask for feedback, and start conversations with people who comment so you both can enjoy learning more!

Collect data. Find out what questions are unanswered about a topic you care about. Research, collect, review, and present the data. Data is powerful, and can change the direction projects take. This could be for a socioeconomic issue, a planned community change, a national problem, or anything that impacts your locality. *Get the facts—and share them!*

Look to Amnesty International, Human Rights Watch, or the United Nations Foundation for ideas on how to advocate for *human rights*.

Start a *petition*. If you want to change something, showing that many people want the change is powerful. Politicians in particular pay attention to petitions because they have the power of numbers behind them!

Contact the media about something good. Media outlets mainly cover negative news events because of public interest, and many "newsworthy" items are not positive. If you know about something positive or inspiring, let the media know! These stories help people feel *upbeat and hopeful* amidst a constant stream of bad news.

Offer to pick up people who want to *vote* but don't have transportation. Regardless of their view, having people involved in the voting process matters. Give them a ride to their polling place so they can participate!

Paint a mural to *lend some beauty* and inspiration to an area. Not an artist? Phone a friend. Find an artistic college student who wants a creative outlet and an amazing resume booster.

Create a *neighborhood watch*. Ask all of your neighbors to be aware of anything unusual. Make sure everyone agrees that "someone who looks different" is not a reason to be concerned: only suspicious activity is cause for alarm. Work together as a team to keep your neighborhood safe!

Remove (negative) *graffiti*.

Support March of Dimes to help prevent premature births. This organization also helps businesses become more mom-friendly, provides research and grants, and helps create policies that *support families* and babies globally. You can donate to help ensure more babies are born healthy! Learn more at MarchofDimes.org.

Help a local orchard *collect fallen apples* at the end of the picking season. These leftover apples are used to make fertilizer for the next season, or as a snack for any animals that live at the orchard.

Distribute a list of resources to *help people in crisis*. Find all the phone numbers and websites for domestic violence victims, for example, and give them to anyone who would come into contact with victims of domestic assault. You can also post these resources online.

Request that diverse and *racially equitable* movies be shown in classes or for groups. Movies that are representative of many groups of people make people feel more welcome and included, and also provide insights into different cultures and beliefs. Tolerance.org offers film kits. Commonsense.org and Edutopia.org also offer dozens of resources for learning that involve diversity. Teachers or facilitators can ask students or participants open-ended questions about their thoughts after the films are shown.

Ask a local *police department* to talk to teens at a high school about how to stay on a successful path.

Join a neighborhood council. Listen, and learn. How can you help? If you're part of the *community voice* and conversation, you know what's happening, and can share that information with others.

Use and understand *bias-free words*. Simply replacing gender-specific words like "fireman" with "firefighter" and using other gender-neutral words is a start. Encourage the use of bias-free words in any organizations you help with.

Host community events for different religious or ethnic holidays, cultures, foods, and popular or historic figures. Help groups you're part of come up with ways to participate, like creating a float for a parade or setting up an activity booth that celebrates a fun and *culturally appropriate* aspect of the community.

Start or join a *PeaceJam* club for teens (PeaceJam.org). This young leaders program works with Nobel Peace Prize winners to help mentor youths in over thirty countries. Teens can attend an event, watch a Nobel Legacy movie, or do an act of peace to help encourage a more peaceful world.

Grow out and donate your hair to make *wigs for kids* who have lost their hair because of alopecia or cancer treatment. Organizations like Wigs for Kids, Children with Hair Loss, and Locks of Love can walk you through the process.

Ask your local restaurants, office cafe, or school cafeteria to offer more *vegetarian, organic, and gluten-free options*. Helping to ensure more people can eat the types of food they prefer creates a healthier, happier community.

Attend a celebration for a religion that is different than yours. Take in all the sights, sounds, and tastes. Every step toward *bridging the gap* between beliefs counts!

Donate *eco-friendly* cleaning products to local shelters.

Learn what the top three or four languages spoken in your region are and learn how to say basic greetings in all of them. Putting forth extra effort to *be friendly* starts any conversation off on the right foot, and shows compassion and a desire to learn more about other cultures.

Connect with "*grandfriends*." A grandfriend is someone from an older generation. These wise, grandparent-aged friends can help make life a little more fun—and impart wisdom you can't get anywhere else. There may be potential grandfriends in your community in assisted-living facilities.

Dine out for a cause. Programs like Dine Out for No Kid Hungry and GroupRaise give money back to causes when you go out to eat. Visit https://dineout.nokidhungry.org or www.groupraise.com/restaurants to discover participating restaurants near you!

Help kids with cancer while teaching kids about *riding safety*. The St. Jude Trike-A-Thon is a service-learning opportunity for daycares and preschools which teaches tricycle and riding-toy safety while raising money to support St. Jude Children's Research Hospital. Teachers or parents can reach out on their website, StJude.org, to help coordinate an event.

Organize a *spay and neuter* event for pets in your area. This service can be offered for a discounted price, or even free, with veterinarians or pet stores as sponsors.

Help parents keep their kids safe by hosting a *safety class* for parents in your neighborhood. You can also ask a police officer to speak in the class.

Keep a few *bird feeders* full of birdseed in a central community area. You can also add some nesting boxes for different species of birds. In cold climates especially, our little bird friends need help with food and shelter.

Virtually *plant a tree*. Many organizations like One Tree Planted, WeForest, and Trees for the Future have programs where you can virtually "plant" trees (which are then physically planted by volunteers). You can also make a donation to a local organization that preserves forest habitats.

Create a *service day* for your neighborhood. In the spring or fall, pick a few neighbors who are elderly or otherwise in need of assistance and help them with completing household chores or with tidying up their yards.

Donate *pool toys* to your local community pool for the children to share and enjoy.

If you speak a second language, offer to *be a translator* at a local museum or nature center. When visitors from other places come to enjoy the sights, they will get a much richer experience if you help them understand some of the unique offerings!

Help a local nonprofit create *voice-overs* for videos or presentations that contain text so more people can enjoy and learn from them.

Have your dog trained as a *"listening dog"* for kids to read to at your local library. This is an easy, low-stress, and fun way for kids to practice reading out loud!

Host a *foreign exchange* student. The student from another country can learn about your country, while you and your family learn about theirs. They will have great experiences to share with others back home, cultivating positive connections between your countries.

Create *hobby kits* for residents of shelters or assisted-living homes. For example, many people enjoy things like knitting, drawing, or painting. Put a few relevant items together in sets for activities that people will enjoy. These can be individual sets, or packs with a dozen of each of the same items that people can enjoy doing together as a group.

Ask a local nursery to donate *holiday-related plants*, trees, or flowers that can then be donated to facilities that temporarily house people (such as shelters, rehabilitation and treatment centers, or hospitals) during the holidays. This will provide a little cheer for anyone who is staying at the facility during those festive times of the year.

Collect unused perfume, makeup, skin care, or *nail care items* for the women (or men) at a local domestic violence shelter.

Have a group you are part of write *kind letters* to seniors. Mail them, or take them to a senior-living facility and read them to the residents.

Hold a free *car wash*. This is a fun activity for school groups to do together, and people in the community will end up with nice, clean cars. You can collect donations too, and give them to a specific cause.

Teach high school students about how loans and credit scores work. These young adults will soon be off to a college or a job, and knowing the basics of *student loans* and good versus bad credit can save them a lot of stress and money down the road.

Sponsor or create a fun *after-dance event* that is drug- and alcohol-free for your local high school.

Grant a wish. **In addition to international organizations like Make-A-Wish that grant big wishes for ill children, there are also regional organizations that provide smaller, more local-based wishes for underserved youths. These can be economical ways for small religious or school groups to give back by providing interesting experiences children would not otherwise have.**

Sponsor a family in another country. Organizations like World Vision, Save the Children, Compassion International, and Unbound have opportunities to sponsor people, as well as information about the impact of sponsorship and details on how to get started.

Hold a local scavenger hunt or *geocaching event*. This can be a great way for people to learn about a neighborhood or park. It can also increase business for an area. A traditional scavenger hunt may have clues to stores, restaurants, or landmarks like statues. Geocaching is similar, but uses GPS coordinates instead.

Host a *bingo night* to get neighbors together. Have local businesses donate some small items for prizes. Small businesses appreciate being associated with positive community events, as these occasions gain publicity and possible tax advantages for their business, and support something people in their own community enjoy.

Raise money to buy *bulletproof vests* for local police dogs. Canine officers need safety equipment too!

Request *bike lanes* be added to high-congestion areas of town so people can safely ride bikes.

Work with your local government officials to plant attractive *native plants* close to highways. When selecting ground cover, consider the special ecological needs for your area by using drought-resistant or fire-resistant plants in dry areas, plants to deter illegal off-road driving in rural areas, or plants that reduce the spread of invasive plants. The areas can be beautiful—and practical!

Collect *old eyeglasses* to be distributed to people in other countries.

Be a *reading tutor* for young kids.

Collect "housewarming" items for local families moving into transitional housing (temporary, low-cost housing, with educational support to help people save money and learn skills that will enable them to eventually get permanent housing). Practical items like towels, dishes, and storage containers, or even decorative items like vases, blankets, or throw pillows can add a *homey touch* in a new environment!

Post a selfie in support of something. Use the cause's or event's *hashtag* in your post.

Encourage teachers at a local school to start the day by sharing positive news stories with their students. Inspirational and educational, these daily discussions will keep kids optimistic and motivated to *share the positivity* with others.

Make first aid kits for residents of *homeless shelters*.

Teach safety classes for *latchkey kids* (kids who are home alone for a couple of hours after school each day while their parents are still at work) so they know what to do in an emergency, including having a list of local emergency contact information and understanding general first aid tips.

Create *public service announcements* (PSAs) on behalf of local nonprofits, and share them with media outlets.

Be a volunteer *tour guide* at a local museum to help people visiting the museum gain a full appreciation of the exhibits.

Organize a parade for a lesser-known historical or cultural event in your hometown. The parade will be both *fun and educational*!

Write a *hometown newsletter* to help everyone stay up to date on everything happening locally. It can be on "traditional" paper or electronic, through email or a website, or even as a page or group on social media.

Ask for additional public restrooms to be built near popular public places in your community so more people can conveniently visit.

Coordinate a cleanup team after an unfortunate act of nature like a flood, wildfire, hurricane, or earthquake. Help your neighborhood (or someone else's neighborhood) get back up and running faster!

Play board or card games with seniors at a senior center.

Write a *grant request* for a nonprofit you support, or participate as a volunteer with United Way in selecting organizations to receive grants (or as part of a committee with a local foundation or nonprofit that grants funds to other organizations).

Host fun activities for *exchange students* from the schools within a moderate driving distance. This will allow the students to meet each other and expand their knowledge of your state, region, and country and its customs.

Create comfort kits or *bedtime bags* for kids affected by natural disasters or homelessness. These can be reusable tote bags with a small cozy blanket, a book to read, a small stuffed animal, warm socks, and a puzzle or toy that is safe for all ages.

Hold a canned *food drive* at a grocery store you frequent. Ask the store to put large cardboard boxes out front so people can buy extras to give on the way out. Donate these canned goods to food pantries in your neighborhood.

Hold a "*snuggle drive.*" Ask friends and neighbors to donate small, new stuffed animals for first responders such as firefighters and police to have handy for children in tough situations.

Create a *prayer or meditation chain* to elevate help for and awareness of an issue. Ask people to sign up for segments of time, like fifteen minutes or an hour, for twenty-four hours total, to pray or meditate on an issue impacting your neighborhood, or the planet. Get some good vibes out there!

Build flower boxes or create *nursery beds* for seniors,
nonprofits, community organizations,
or anyone else in your area who could use some
extra beauty.

Become a volunteer *lifeguard* at a
community pool or camp.

Create a list of local, free *learning resources* for
your community. Share it with organizations that
interact with people who might benefit from classes,
certifications, or trade skills. Some organizations,
such as big-box stores, community colleges, libraries,
universities, and nonprofits, often offer free training or
classes both in person and online.

Create "chemo care kits" for children going through cancer treatment. Organizations like Lemons of Love and Chemo Comfort can help coordinate this, or you can gift knitted or fleece hats, cozy socks, lightweight blankets, and cheerful pillowcases to brighten patients' days. There are also many premade kits you can order online, then deliver to a local hospital.

Create a *giving tree*. This can be connected to a holiday or a season. Find out what some families in your area need, and write all of the items on cutout ornaments, flowers, leaves, or pieces of paper. Anyone can take one of the cutouts and purchase the item listed to donate to the project.

Join a *bone marrow* registry. Bone marrow transplants can be lifesaving treatments for leukemia, lymphoma, and other diseases. It only takes a minute to register, and in the event that you become a match, your donation could save someone's life and have a ripple effect not only for that person, but also for their family and friends.

During the holidays, have older kids help with a *gift-wrapping table* in a popular shopping area. Use recycled materials or reusable gift bags. Ask people to make an optional small donation to use to buy toys for needy kids. Free gift-wrapping saves stress for people, and kids will get some new toys too!

Keep *reusable tote bags* in your car to use instead of plastic bags. Reusable tote bags are also great for many types of donation kits for homeless shelters, etc.

If you have input in the *programming* that people are watching on TV, like in waiting rooms or community centers, put positive, educational, or comedy programs on instead of the news. The news can be heavily negative, lowering people's spirits.

Ask your local middle school what *novels* the students are reading this year. Then, get some people together to donate several dozen copies of each book for their school library, or for each child to keep.

Create a framed *Google Earth* photo of your neighborhood or city with *landmarks* highlighted to give to local establishments. That way, they can let people know about other interesting places to visit in your hometown, which will keep visitors—and their friends and family—coming back to both the area and the store.

Ask a local *radio station* or TV talk show to discuss an important topic so more people can hear about it and get involved. Offer to help find experts on the topic for interviews. Or offer to be interviewed if you have expertise!

Make *pet disaster kits* to donate to a local pet shelter, and be sure to make them for your pets too. When a natural disaster hits, pets need help along with people. A backup leash, food, basic first aid supplies, and pet safety information can be included in the kits. Keep those happy tails wagging!

Be a *"grannie"* or *"grandad"* for less fortunate children in India, Greenland, Mexico, or Colombia as part of School in the Cloud's program. You can read, sing, and talk with these children so they can have a warm experience with other people around the globe, and feel more like a part of the global family!

Get a group to sponsor a billboard in a high-traffic area to share information on an important subject.

Create disaster-zone maps for nonprofits. Often when natural or other disasters strike, it is a challenge for nonprofits to get to people who need help. Using satellite images, you can help map roads, rivers, buildings, and other landmarks to help responders find their way. The Humanitarian OpenStreetMap Team is one organization you can work with to help. Learn more at Hotosm.org.

Play *Foldit* to help discover new scientific breakthroughs. *Foldit* is a computer puzzle game that contributes to scientific research. By solving puzzles, you might be uncovering a key component needed to help medical research progress toward a new cure!

Help a nonprofit plan an event. A well-produced event gets the community involved in and aware of all the good work an organization does. So, if you have any planning skills, contacts, or resources to provide, *lending a hand* can make a big difference for a favorite cause. Even contacting guests or assembling materials is valuable!

Examine *cyclones* online to help predict activity in the future. The more precise historical records of cyclones are, the more useful they are for future predictions. If you'd like to help the millions affected by cyclones each year, you can visit CycloneCenter.org to lend your eyes to the project.

Help someone you know who doesn't have *health insurance* get enrolled in any insurance programs that offer free or reduced healthcare costs. Insurance may be expensive, but not having it can be catastrophic if an emergency or severe illness happens.

Find a *cure* for cancer by playing games like *Cancer Crusade* online. *Citizen Science Games* features games used to crowdsource real scientific research. Try your hand at it—you might help save lives!

Join in your United Way chapter's *Day of Caring*, or a similar annual day of volunteering organized by a nonprofit. These events bring dozens or hundreds of volunteers together to go out into the community to help local nonprofits with one-time projects. Typical projects include tidying up a ballpark, repairing and painting fences, constructing accessibility ramps, washing windows and walls, or doing anything administrative that nonprofits need, and all of the necessary items to complete the project are provided.

Deliver *fresh produce* to a local shelter.

Code for a cause. Do you have some *coding skills*? Or maybe app development skills? Search online for "code for good," and you'll discover many ways to join hackathons or groups that hold challenges to create tools that help the greater good.

Donate extra *estate items* (and save costs on junk removal services). Organizations like Goodwill and The Salvation Army offer services where they will come clear out an estate for a modest donation fee.

Train your dog to be a *therapy dog*. With a little instruction, dogs can be certified to go to hospitals, hospices, senior-living homes, and other places to cheer people up and help them relax and smile.

Help the *LGBTQ community* have a more positive and inclusionary voice in media. Through organizations like GLAAD and your own local media, you can make sure the narrative and imagery used to discuss and portray LGBTQ people is positive.

Learn to say some common *travel phrases* in multiple languages, especially if you're traveling to a different country. Also, learn a few conversational phrases (and responses!) if you want to chat with anyone. Asking locals about their city and country while traveling can give you interesting stories to share with people back home, and a deeper appreciation of others!

Ask local *wildlife rescue* experts to hold an educational event so homeowners know what to do and who to contact if a wild animal is injured or is causing a problem such as threatening residents or destroying property.

Hold a community *bake-off* contest. Have a few modest prizes and awards for the winners. Auction all of the baked goods off at the end and award the proceeds to a local cooking or baking program for underserved youths.

Move with purpose. CharityMiles.org lets people *"move with purpose"* by accumulating money per mile biked, walked, or run that can be donated to charity. If you are exercising anyway, why not let more people reap the benefits?

Volunteer as a team to help the blind or *visually impaired*. The app Be My Eyes allows you to use live video chats to help low-vision and blind people complete daily tasks.

Update or create a *Wikipedia* page. *Wikipedia* is an open-source encyclopedia created by and for everyone. Anyone can create pages by registering, and anyone can edit pages. So, if you have knowledge about something interesting or *world changing*, let your global community know!

Have an ongoing *book drive* at your place of work to collect books for all ages. Donate them to organizations that shelter or otherwise care for the less fortunate.

Help stray cats by providing *outdoor shelters* (a large plastic bin with a cover and a square hole cut into one side works well) with food and water, and contacting a local animal rescue. You can also report them as "found" with posts and pictures on social media, in case they are a lost pet.

Donate or raise money for a "group toy" to be used in a community center or other location where many people can enjoy it. *Group toys* include items for game rooms or recreation rooms like ping-pong tables, pool tables, foosball, shuffleboard, or magnetic dartboard sets.

Add *errands* for others when you're already out and about. Keep a list of things needed regularly by local nonprofits, or elderly neighbors, and as you go about your own errands, grab a few of those things.

Ask community or government buildings to add *healthy choices* in any vending machines that serve the public. Each additional healthy choice made individually adds up to a healthier community!

Donate photos to CreativeCommons.org. Creative Commons is a free database of photos donated by the global community and available for use by anyone. There are different levels of use. If you have photos that might *inspire action* or create emotion, donate them for free use by nonprofits and others.

Clown around for kids. Comic Relief has an annual Red Nose Day event to raise donations for kids around the world. You can purchase a red clown nose to make a donation, then wear it in photos to share with your friends and family on social media and inspire others to get involved.

Create safe environments on college campuses. Make sure sexual assault is not acceptable by using the free tools on ItsonUs.org. You can download their Consent Discussion Guide, host an event to talk to peers and friends about what *consent* means, or make a creative public service announcement (PSA) to share using their provided script. Because stopping sexual assault is on all of us!

Create a "*random acts of kindness*" board for a classroom or group. Come up with a few dozen simple acts that are safe and age appropriate for the group involved. Print out the ideas on paper or cardboard and put them into envelopes or containers attached to the board. Have group members select one act per day or week to do collectively, or have each person pick one to do individually.

Talk to a local committee about taking steps to ensure that they are representing *diversity* that reflects the backgrounds and needs of the area.

Support "*buy one, give one*" companies when purchasing things. Companies like TOMS shoes and Warby Parker glasses provide one pair of their products to someone in need for each pair sold.

Solicit grocers or farmers' markets to move into areas in your community that are currently "food deserts," where it is a challenge to find *healthy food* choices.

Create prayer blankets or lap shawls for the elderly. This is a fun group project, and the items can be donated to a place of worship, senior center, community center, or shelter to add a little warmth to someone's day!

Create "birthday bags" with items for a child's birthday, like candles, cake mix, frosting, balloons, and simple gift-wrapping supplies, to donate to food pantries. If someone in need has a birthday coming up, they will be able to have a nice celebration.

Attend presentations by speakers who have different viewpoints than yours, and bring a few friends. The world is changed by intelligent people being open-minded when listening to other people's views.

Dress up the *teachers' lounge* at your child's school. This can be undertaken as a class project, or with a group of parents. Provide a fresh paint job, new chairs or tables, or tableware—such as ceramic mugs, cups, plates, bowls, or silverware—as needed. Teachers change the world every day by helping kids learn, so show your appreciation!

Ask people to buy a box of cute *Band-Aids* the next time they go to the drugstore. Once you've collected a few dozen boxes, donate them to a local charity or medical center that serves kids. A little smile after a boo-boo can make all the difference to a child.

Do you have a business with a wholesale license, or the ability to *buy in bulk*? If you do, purchase a large volume of small toys (appropriate for most ages) and donate them to nonprofits or schools that have fairs or other events with games and prizes.

Leave some *change or dollar bills* behind in areas where they will be a pleasant surprise to someone. Good spaces include vending machine coin returns, laundromat dryers, park benches, and parking spaces.

Keep information real. The work of Craig Newmark Philanthropies, established by *craigslist* founder Craig Newmark, supports organizations and causes tied to independence and truth in journalism, voting rights, and efforts that support military veterans and women in technology. These are areas that, when given the opportunity, universally contribute to *positive changes* in the world! Organizations with a similar focus can apply for grants.

Help a Reporter Out. HARO is an organization that helps provide sources for *journalists*. Journalists will request experts or sources on topics, and you can offer to be one of those resources by answering questions and providing your information. Your help makes it that much easier for journalists to get the facts on things that are happening in the world, and to inform the public.

Promote *common spaces* like parks, libraries, beaches, or public squares by holding group events there, using them regularly yourself, and telling others about them. When people spend time in public spaces, they not only connect with others and enjoy their communities, but also encourage future funding and expansion by showing that people appreciate the value of the spaces.

Be sensitive to cultural appropriation in everything you do. Don't repurpose important pieces of culture for uses that don't uplift the culture, especially when planning events. Instead, ask friends from those different cultures for ideas about food, music, and décor that are a real, an authentic, and an accurate and *positive representation* of their customs or holidays. Highlighting other cultures and their specific arts, norms, traditions, and other elements is a positive way to change the world!

Provide meals to people who are too sick or immobile to shop or cook for themselves. Volunteer for Meals on Wheels (www.mealsonwheelsamerica.org) to help deliver *free or low-cost meals* to elderly people who are homebound. Looking for an international chapter? You can also search Meals on Wheels in your region for information on your nearest Meals on Wheels location.

Be a "safe sleep hero" and make sure all the babies in your life wake up after every nap or bedtime. Make sure new parents and grandparents know the latest science of *safe sleep*: ABCD. Babies need to sleep Alone (nothing at all in or on the sides of the crib, including stuffed animals or blankets), on their Back, in a Crib, and Don't ever smoke (or use drugs or alcohol) around a baby.

Help create a local seed library. *Seed libraries* are places where people can get seeds to grow plants, and then give back seeds from those plants for others to use. Some traditional libraries offer these, as do nature centers and parks.

Use a special occasion to *help others*. The next time you have a birthday, wedding shower, baby shower, anniversary, or another special occasion where gifts might be expected, ask people to donate to a charity instead, or donate the gifts you get to an organization that can steward them to people who need them more.

Donate to a pet shelter in remembrance of a *beloved pet*. When a pet dies, it is heartbreaking. One way to help your furry family member's memory live on is to make a donation of money or of their items to a pet shelter. Organizations like Golden Retrievers in Need Rescue Service and The Pet Fund help owners take care of their pets, while keeping the memory of your departed friend alive.

Round up for good. Apps like MyChange and Bstow let you make small donations regularly just by using your *debit or credit card*. When you make a purchase, the price you pay can be automatically rounded up to the nearest dollar and donated to your selected charity.

Use your inspiration for good when reading about positive things. *Action Button* by Speakable lets you take action, like donating, emailing policy makers, or signing petitions, on articles you read. If you feel inspired to act from reading an article, you can, right then and there!

Be a "*placemaker*." Placemaking is the idea of creating more useful areas out of unused or underutilized public spaces. Those spaces could be neglected parks, plazas, or even vacant lots. With a little collaborative planning, these spaces can be reimagined into gardens, playgrounds, museums, recreation areas, or other things that the community will enjoy.

Create a *free pantry*. It can be for canned goods, toiletries, socks, undergarments, or something else your community members need. You can set up your pantry in places like on the grounds of a local place of worship, or close to an elementary school. Ask people you know to give items to the pantry, and let nonprofits know where it is and what items people might find there.

Give to the pets of elderly people. While seniors have some options to help themselves as far as food goes, often their *companion animals* do not. So the pets of seniors can end up in shelters when times get tough. Help prevent seniors from losing their pet companions by donating pet food and supplies to senior centers.

Ask a local college or university's school of social work if they have a few students who can help a local nonprofit with brainstorming ideas or carrying out events. This provides the students with *real-life experience* and benefits the community that the students are helping in.

Help a local nursery or greenhouse create *workshops for kids*. Learning how to grow things and maintain healthy ecosystems are valuable lessons for the future of any community.

Create something unusual to share your views on an important issue. Board games, cartoons, plays, songs, poems, art, and other *interesting mediums* help grab people's attention better than the traditional dull pamphlets or speeches. Make sure your voice is heard so that more people can help you create positive change!

Join the global change movement by phone. GlobalCitizen.org has petitions and pre-written *Twitter tweets* that you can sign and share with one click. Combining your voice with thousands of others creates a message that will really be heard.

Be a college *hometown ambassador*. Toward the end of college or university, offer to go back to your hometown to talk about the program you're in with high school students who are considering similar programs in the near future. Share information about what you're studying and what careers it prepares you for, and answer any questions they have. Hearing positive things from someone who is actually in a program will inspire others to take that next step and enroll!

Read to children waiting for doctors' appointments. Kids will enjoy being read to while they wait to see a doctor or nurse, and the fun distraction will help to relax them in an often scary environment.

Volunteer as a group exercise instructor. With some basic training and occasionally a certification, you can lead groups in *exercise classes* like yoga, water aerobics, spinning, or tai chi. Many senior centers and local community centers offer these classes.

Teach a *test preparation* workshop for a school diploma or work certification program. Many literacy programs offer training options to volunteers so they can learn how to teach groups how to study for and pass important diploma or certification tests.

Participate as a volunteer for free *health screenings* in your area. Assist with tasks like helping people to find where to go, handing out information, and checking people in.

Create a *food bags program* for a local school. Many kids who get food at school may not have access to the same quantity of healthy food on weekends or during school breaks. Keep kids healthy and fed all year long!

Set up plastic bag *recycling boxes* at the entrances of local grocery stores so that plastic bags can be recycled more easily by your community. More than five hundred billion plastic bags are used globally each year. Reusing or recycling existing plastic bags keeps them out of landfills and the oceans.

Buy garage sale furniture that is sturdy, and donate it to a local shelter for use by people moving into transitional housing. Many nonprofit organizations that work with the homeless or victims of domestic violence need basic *home furnishings*. You can also let your neighbors know about this idea for when they are updating their home furnishings and have a few good items to donate.

Help people process grief. *Grief center* volunteers help provide resources, referrals, support, and education for people during times of bereavement and loss.

Ask a local school to donate their leftover *cafeteria food* to a homeless shelter.

Offer to change batteries in your neighbors' *smoke detectors*. You can also donate batteries for use in smoke detectors to your local fire department or Red Cross chapter, who may already give away free smoke detectors.

Nominate a few *world-changers* for local, regional, national, or international recognition and awards. Find nonprofit or community contests, and recommend people from your area who do good on a regular basis, in small or large ways. This is a great way to reward positive action in your community!

Let the #hashtags guide your way. If you have an interest in helping your community in a specific way, search those hashtags on social media, along with your city name. For example, *Twitter* advanced search lets you look for *#volunteering* with #pets in #yourhometown. Anyone having a conversation about those topics will show up for you to see in real time, so you can easily find opportunities.

Facilitate *meetings*. Many organizations need skilled facilitators to turn their ideas for community action and engagement into reality. So, if you have a gift for running meetings or workshops, make a future meeting fun—and productive.

Take healthy "snack packs" to after-school clubs or sports events for the club or team. *Fuel creativity* (and kids)!

Supply shoes. In many countries, children don't go to school because they don't have shoes. Many organizations like Soles4Souls accept actual shoes as donations, or money can be donated to organizations like Hope Runs to provide *shoes for children*. If your old running shoes are too dilapidated to donate, companies like Nike and Converse will accept them at many stores globally and recycle them to be used to make new shoes.

Walk kids home from school. If you live in an area where kids often walk home, gather some friends together and create a program to *walk kids home*, ensuring that they arrive safely.

Build an inclusive and *accessible playground*. Could your neighborhood, school, or community center use some playground fun that friends with disabilities can enjoy? Modifications like handrails, ramps, and braille instructions make playground equipment more accessible to kids with functional needs. There are nonprofit organizations like KaBOOM! that specialize in creating playgrounds that are inclusive for functional needs, and many local community organizations may offer small grants to help with accessible upgrades or equipment.

Help people bundle up. If your region experiences cold weather, there are people in need of warm winter coats. Place cardboard boxes at participating businesses or in school classrooms to *collect coats* for those who may not be able to afford them.

Give the pediatric wing of your local hospital a library. Collect books from friends and neighbors, build or buy a bookshelf that works for the hospital's available space, and set up a *cozy library* for kids to enjoy!

Get crafty. Gather up *craft supplies* for classrooms, community centers, playrooms, or childcare centers. Check first to see what is age appropriate for the place receiving the supplies, then collect or buy crayons, markers, safety scissors, construction paper, stickers, sponges and paintbrushes, watercolor or acrylic paint, school glue or glue sticks, felt, ribbons, and other supplies to donate.

Be a *helpful snacker*. Whenever you see a bake sale, buy a few items for yourself—and a few items to give to friends and relatives. When you give away the treats, let the receiver know about the organization and how they can donate or get involved.

Collect *pull tabs* from aluminum soda cans for charity. This is an easy group project that school classes and youth groups can participate in to feel more engaged in helping. Ronald McDonald House, an international organization that helps families stay close to children during medical crises, uses donated pull tabs to support their house operations.

Help an organization make their documents digital. Anyone can help *scan documents* or input data for organizations. Once data is digital, it saves the organization a lot of staff time searching for, organizing, and using those documents. That time can then be spent on other, more mission-critical work.

Be a volunteer "friendly visitor." Sometimes, a simple smile and a friendly chat are just what the doctor ordered. See if a local senior center or community center could use someone to walk around greeting people, striking up some friendly conversations, and *sharing smiles* along the way.

Staff an *information booth* at a local health, nonprofit, or political event. You'll have a chance to connect with dozens or even hundreds of community members, as well as learn more about different local organizations.

Attend a "*poverty simulation.*" These events aim to show people what everyday life is like for someone below the poverty line. Participants have restrictions around income, transportation, medical care, food, housing, employment, and more for a set time period.

Be a summer camp volunteer. A great match for teenagers, *summer camp volunteering* combines the outdoors with fun adventures and new friends. Summer camp volunteers not only get to try new activities and learn leadership skills, but also help members of their community do the same—all while making fun summer memories!

Donate food, pet supplies, or money to *pet food banks*. Pets are members of the family. But when times get hard, sometimes pets get separated from their families because there aren't enough resources to go around. Help keep animals and their families together with a simple donation.

Host a monthly *birthday party* for all of the kids with birthdays that month who are part of a shelter, youth group, or community center. Bring along some friends, decorations, treats, and fun activities to give extra cheer to the birthday kids.

Be a volunteer *firefighter*. Volunteer firefighting is a great way to serve your community. There are also other jobs at local firehouses, like maintaining vehicles and managing office tasks, which contribute to keeping people in your community safe.

Teach kids how to interact with *service animals*. Because service dogs are medically necessary and can be lifesaving, they need to stay focused and attentive. Many children are unaware that the best thing to do is to politely ignore service animals, since they are actively working to help their owner, even if it looks like they aren't. It's important that kids avoid things such as petting, touching, talking, getting too close, whistling, touching their equipment, or engaging in any other interaction. Yes, service animals are adorable, but they are also busy being heroes!

Speak more than one language? Offer to *translate in hospitals* for parents whose children are patients. It can be a challenging time when a child is sick, and being able to ask questions or make sure you properly understand the directions for care is critical.

Start a book club within an organization. This will better engage the people they work with, and *build literacy* and camaraderie.

Adopt something special in your hometown as a team or group. It could be a road median, a bench, a flower bed, a monument, or a busy corner. Work together to maintain the spot on a regular basis and fix it when necessary.

Set the table. Any organization that regularly feeds large numbers of people can use volunteers to help set things up ahead of time. In addition to serving food, you could also set up dining areas for individual place settings or buffet service.

Show people a good time. Help your *local theater* by collecting tickets, ushering people to their seats, or running a concession stand to make a performance even more special for everyone.

Set up *playdates*—big ones. Work with an organization to prepare space needed for a childcare facility, and find other volunteers to help provide daycare.

Let people's creativity—and feelings—shine with *art therapy*. Art therapy can help people with things such as trauma, addiction, grief and loss, depression, and anxiety. Art therapy organizations like the International Expressive Arts Therapy Association and Art Therapy Without Borders can give you guidance for how to lead different types of art therapy.

Freecycle. Freecycling is giving away or trading something no longer of value to someone else who will enjoy it. One person's trash is another person's treasure! If there isn't a freecycling group in your area, start one.

Teach driver's education. With some training and licensing, you can help create *safe drivers* within your community!

Donate coupons. Military families can use even expired coupons overseas. Food and baby supply coupons are needed the most. An easy group project, *clipping coupons* can get your whole family or class involved in doing something simple that can make the difference for others.

Sort books at the library. Local libraries can use extra hands to help with things like sorting and reshelving returned books, or sorting book donations.

Get on board with Giving Tuesday. An international sensation, *#GivingTuesday* started online as a day to give back during the holiday shopping insanity that takes place during the winter. You can make a few quick donations online, share stories from favorite nonprofits with friends, or volunteer. It's the Tuesday after American Thanksgiving, usually in late November or the first week of December.

Be a *crossing guard*. Help kids cross roads and intersections to and from school safely.

Handwrite letters to politicians. Gather up some kindred spirits and send a politician a message of support or disagreement. In a sea of emails, calls, or texts, good *old-fashioned letters* can really stand out. Send them individually as part of a group project, or have people sign a few cards or letters together.

Chaperone a school *field trip*. You can help all the kids feel comfortable and stay safe, all while they learn about something new and interesting!

Adopt a family for a holiday. Provide a holiday meal, or supplies for smaller meals for a week, to a family in need during the *holiday season*.

Give your old electronics new homes. Donate any unused (and working) *electronics* such as TVs, DVD players, stereos, tablets, gaming systems, and computers to local schools, libraries, shelters, or community centers. There, they can be enjoyed by many members of the community, even if they aren't the latest version!

Create a summer program for schoolchildren to *encourage reading* over the school break. Kids can keep track of the books they read and win prizes if they hit a certain goal. Prizes can be gift certificates for treats like pizza, or fun little knickknacks like finger puppets.

Clean a stream. A river or stream can accumulate debris and garbage on its banks. Gather a group together to spend a few hours picking up trash and recyclables so your community can enjoy the stream's original, pristine *natural beauty*.

Spruce up a hiking trail. Hiking is a tactile way for community members to *experience nature*. With permission from the park or landowner, add a wooden bench, mile markers, or a small plaque highlighting an interesting history or nature fact to a trail.

Shed some light on the subject. Let your local government know about any locations in your community that could use *streetlights* for better visibility and safety at night.

Get your community outside with a little paint. Find smooth river rocks that are a few inches wide, and paint them. They can have uplifting quotes, cute pictures, or simple ways for the finder to make their own *difference* in the world. When people find them, they can post photos to social media along with the location where they found the rock, and hide it again for someone else to find. This is fun and uplifting way to get people outdoors!

Host a basic *home-maintenance* class for your neighbors or at a community center. This is an easy way to save time and money on simple household needs, and neighbors who have these skills can help other neighbors when they need it.

Hold a creative demonstration. Sure, the standard march with signs is a solid choice, but there are other ways to make your voice heard! Stage a large number of items that represent your cause in a *creative* way (think construction hard hats for labor, tennis balls for dogs, buckets for water—anything unique with a tie to the issue).

Make blank *greeting cards* and deliver them to a shelter or senior-living facility for visitors to write words of encouragement on and give to the residents.

Teach or organize a class for your community on how to make eco-friendly and cost-saving homemade *household necessities* like laundry detergent, spray cleaner, sunscreen, bug spray, shampoo, and hand soap.

Host a group *scrapbooking* class. This is a great way to put memories together to look at easily. With some bulk materials such as basic scrapbooks, glue, scissors, decorative papers, and small accessories (try deep discount stores and clearance sections) and each participant's own favorite photos, everyone can leave with a cherished book of happy memories!

Hold a sit-in or lie-in to make a *social justice* point. Be sure to get required permissions and permits in advance.

Create a neighborhood *emergency plan*. Make copies of the neighborhood plan, along with a checklist for a two-day emergency supply kit, and give copies to your neighbors or your local government office for them to distribute and put online.

Run for office. If you think things could be done a better way, give it a shot!

Help a nonprofit or cultural organization create a diversity and *inclusion policy* so more community voices can be actively heard!

Work with your local school system to create additional *volunteering opportunities* on nights and weekends for those parents who aren't able to volunteer during school days.

If you are an entrepreneur, host a discussion at your workplace to talk about diversity, gender equity, and the creation of a *bias-free environment*. Make sure that everyone with something to say, or an idea for making the company more inclusive and bias-free, is given a chance to be heard.

Do a random act of kindness for three people, and suggest that they *pay it forward* to three more people. The ripple effect adds up fast!

Crochet or knit blankets, hats, scarves, or mittens to donate. Shelters and their residents will appreciate the warmth and care of a *homemade knit*.

Refer someone to 211. United Way's free phone hotline, 2-1-1, is confidential and available twenty-four hours a day. Trained staff connect people to resources in their area, such as food, housing, medical services, veterans' programs, crisis centers, disaster and emergency services, and more. These services are also available at 211.org. For international hotlines, simply web-search your region's helpline number to refer a friend, family member, or neighbor.

Teach a young adult about compound interest. Albert Einstein called compound interest "the greatest mathematical discovery of all time" for good reason. If a young adult understands that starting his or her investing for retirement at age twenty-five instead of age thirty-five will result in almost twice as much money by age sixty-five, it can have a positive lifelong effect for them and their family. The learning website KhanAcademy.org has easy-to-follow videos on compound interest.

Double the smiles. One way to create more overall impact is by connecting two groups together who *mutually benefit*. For example, schoolchildren can decorate place mats for homebound people who receive Meals on Wheels, or make no-sew blankets for organizations like Project Linus, which gives blankets to children in need. The kids will love the fun of creating things, as well as the joy of giving, and the recipients will enjoy their creations!

Help a *refugee family* in your hometown. People seeking the safety of a new country may need help with locating language resources, finding employment, navigating healthcare, getting children enrolled in schools, finding housing, and connecting with many other things we take for granted. The International Rescue Committee has numerous ways to help—just visit Rescue.org to get started!

Double the impact of your donations. Are you an employee whose company will match your nonprofit donations? According to DoubletheDonation.com, between six and ten billion dollars of matching gift money is left unused each year. Remember to ask for the *matching gift* when you make a donation, so your favorite cause gets twice the money. Help even more by asking your HR team to send reminders to all employees about requesting matching donations.

Become an organization's *number one fan*. The power of sharing and awareness can go a long way toward helping a favorite local organization do more in your community. If you have social media accounts, like or follow your favorite organization or nonprofit, and share their interesting activities and events with your network on a regular basis. Also, be sure to tell people in person—or via email or text—when you hear about something fun the organization is doing!

Be a liaison between exchange students and a local organization, senior center, or government entity to help the exchange students present information about their homeland to the group members. This encourages both volunteerism for the exchange student and *international appreciation* by the members of the group who get to meet the student. Listeners walk away with a newfound appreciation for another culture and country, as well as a personal experience with someone who actually is from there!

Give world-changing gifts. Don't know what to get someone? Try passes for *educational experiences*—museums, aquariums, arboretums, and zoos. Annual family memberships are perfect for families with kids (or kids at heart). Fun family time coupled with new knowledge and experiences with plants, animals, art, and the environment helps create inspiration and a world-changing sense of adventure!

Support public broadcast media. *Public media* in free countries tends to have a more neutral, educational focus. It is also at least partly funded by public donations.

Create a *meditation group*. Meditation creates a sense of focus and peace. It's been shown to increase concentration, improve happiness, and reduce stress. The calming effects can help create greater harmony within communities, one group at a time!

Volunteer with the *Peace Corps*. Check out PeaceCorps.gov for more information on all of the ways you can help!

Take a *conflict resolution* course, then teach one. Not only can you be helpful in contentious situations if they arise, but you can also help others learn how to better listen to the perspectives of others and defuse tense situations.

Share your ideas about *human rights* with others! Try your hand (or encourage a young person you know to try their hand) at storytelling for good by entering song lyrics, photographs, or an article on an interesting facet of human rights into the Amnesty International Youth Awards. Enter at www.amnesty.org/en.

Ask public systems to switch their buildings over to at least partial *solar power*. They will be able to reduce electricity costs—and be kind to the environment.

If the company you work for uses company cars, ask them to purchase *hybrid vehicles* as older vehicles age out of the fleet. Electric vehicles are a good option too.

Help kids make "*helping calendars.*" Simply add set times to volunteer or give back to the community to a special calendar, and add gold stars when a service is completed. Kids will develop a habit of giving, while enjoying their role in creating a calendar of helpful activities.

Take a group tour of a *recycling plant.* Listen to the interesting information about how the process works and what it takes to make something new instead of reusing or recycling. This can have a strong impact on kids in particular, as they realize how much better it is to be mindful of what they throw away.

If you are a member of the LGBTQ community, consider a volunteer vacation specifically designed to show the world how much of a positive impact the *LGBTQ community* makes on the globe. Groups like Global Volunteers offer volunteering trips with other LGBTQ travelers. It's a peaceful and productive way to show humanity and connectedness in a safe and inclusive environment.

Pitch a *social enterprise* idea. Social enterprises combine business with social impact. Create a plan to help change the world, and let investors know what it is! Your idea might be the next big thing to change the world.

Teach your kids to *compliment people* and say "thank you" often. Whether expressed with spoken words, with a note, through a generous tip, or in a thoughtful small gesture, compliments and gratitude benefit both the giver and receiver each time.

Ask your company executives to *incorporate giving* into the mission statement and vision of the company. If giving is emphasized in this way, it can open the door to new actions such as allowing employees more time to volunteer, making more donations to nonprofits, and getting employees involved in awareness projects like charity walks and charity teams.

Hold a *yoga event*. The event can be held simply for community and the creation of a sense of calm and serenity, or in support of something like peace or human rights. Never underestimate the power of positive thinking and mindfulness— especially in groups!

Hold a *trivia competition* for a nonprofit. The trivia can have a theme, such as history or movies, or contain a mix of different topics. The community will enjoy the educational fun of the competition, while the nonprofit will be able to get their name and mission out there.

Tell a nonprofit you know about *Google Ad Grants*. Through Google Ad Grants, Google awards up to $10,000 in Google AdWords advertising each month—for free. This can help the organization be more visible when people are searching for help online. Check out www.google.com/grants for details.

Attend *town hall* meetings. Participate in what decisions are being made in your community!

At the next event you attend, grab unused paper napkins and *disposable cutlery* that would otherwise be thrown away. Donate these items to places like shelters and to nonprofit events that serve food.

Think about diversity when organizing events, including speaker choices, locations, food choices, accessibility, and other often-overlooked areas where proactively choosing more diversity can make a big impact. More people may attend and feel included if an effort is made to be diverse and inclusive from the beginning.

Talk to your employer about providing *positive wellness classes* like yoga, mindfulness, or meditation for employees. Another option is allowing employees to earn wellness points to exchange for discounts on their insurance premiums.

Start a "*compliment campaign*" with a group of friends to compliment every person you meet for a week. Write about how people responded, and share the story as a challenge for others.

Be a *team captain* for a local charity walk. In addition to recruiting people to walk and raising some money for a cause, you can use the opportunity to wear a crazy costume (capes, anyone?) to highlight your own organization to the other walkers.

Participate in a *social media* challenge. The ALS Ice Bucket Challenge raised more than $115 million globally for amyotrophic lateral sclerosis. When you spot a fun, safe challenge for a cause you like, go for it! Be sure to post it online and ask others to do it; the power of a social media campaign is its ability to spread through personal networks.

Participate in a safe *research study* to help researchers learn more. That additional information could be just the thing needed to make a breakthrough!

Help *runaways*. November is National Runaway Prevention Month in the United States, but runaways need help all year round. Aid in a community program that helps runaways through counseling, housing, or substance abuse treatment. If your community doesn't have any programs for runaways, start one!

Be early. Being fifteen minutes early to any meeting shows *respect* for other people's time, and encourages others to do the same.

Get passports for yourself and your family. Having passports ready to go opens the door to adventures and world-changing *new experiences* with other cultures.

Introduce *meditation classes* for incarcerated youths, or for schoolkids instead of detentions. Research has shown positive results from kids learning to control their thoughts and reactions better through the calming practices of meditation.

Model *positive behaviors*, like reading, healthy eating, and exercising, to children. The simple act of leading by example has powerful effects on how kids perceive things like right and wrong.

Ask local medical practices and hospitals to start offering *telemedicine* so that more people—including those with limited access to transportation, work schedule challenges, or mobility problems—can have access to quality medical care.

Hold a community *dog wash* where four-legged friends can get a bath in exchange for a small donation, such as dog food, supplies, toys, or cash, that will be donated to a local animal shelter. Take lots of pictures for social media, and include a link on each one to the animal shelter's donation page to really compound the donations from all of those adorable pooches!

If you're a woman, contribute to information websites like *Quora* and *Reddit*. Having more women contributors helps ensure a more balanced view of topics.

Post flyers with helpful resources for youth issues like bullying and LGBTQ safety in places where youths will see them.

Join or create an election technology collaborative or cooperative to find and make better ways to get the word out, and activate people, for voting.

Help a teacher get a *small grant* for something his or her classroom needs. Check out DonorsChoose.org or NGOSource.org for more information!

Help a school become a certified *Schoolyard Habitat* through the National Wildlife Federation (NWF.org). Kids can get involved by planning and creating ways to provide food, water, and shelter for local wildlife, as well as ways to use the space for teaching.

Volunteer as a family or a group in the Special Olympics. The *Special Olympics* holds tens of thousands of events around the world each year! You can cheer in the stands, coach, or participate in unified sports teams alongside people with intellectual disabilities. Visit SpecialOlympics.org to discover all the ways to get involved.

Hold youth workshops where young people get together to discuss important issues and brainstorm their own creative ways to address them. Smart, passionate young people are even more empowered to create *impactful change* when they are involved in the process of understanding problems and designing solutions. The ability to think about issues in this way is a skill that helps create future leaders!

Educate people on the connection between legislation and policy, and how it impacts their daily lives. The more people know about the effect *policies and laws* have on them—good or bad—the more likely they are to get involved. You can make a quick explainer video, infographic, or blog post about why a proposed law is important and how it affects you and your neighbors.

Prevent "*compassion fatigue*" with supporters when doing fundraising or advocacy campaigns. Compassion fatigue is an indifference to appeals for help that happens when people are asked to help too often, or are asked by too many organizations. Provide people with a productive and positive call to action, including ways to help other than donating, along with inspiring testimonials. Highlight powerful stories, and include an example of a simple act someone can take to help them feel empowered to make a difference.

Give kids a creative outlet by enlisting their help with set designs and promotional posters for local plays and *theater productions*.

Check out Dolly Parton's *Imagination Library* and start one in your hometown. This program delivers one free book each month to kids from their birth to age five!

Test your home for lead paint, and have loved ones and neighbors test their homes too. Homes built before 1978 (in the United States) may have *lead paint*. Lead is especially dangerous to pregnant women and young children. If your home tests positive for lead paint, be sure to have the affected components professionally abated or removed.

If you volunteer or work with any *underprivileged groups*, ask them about their hopes, dreams, and ideas, rather than simply "prescribing" a solution you think will help them. The term "parachuting in" refers to a nonprofit going in to a community with good intentions, but without listening to what that community is already doing for themselves, or what they want for themselves. Listening to the people most impacted by problems—and potential solutions—is a powerful way to make sure good intentions turn into good outcomes for the people being served.

Help create a healthy cooking *show-and-tell* in a classroom. Provide packages of healthy premeasured ingredients along with a recipe for the kids. Ask them to cook or bake the recipes together with their family, then bring in a story or photo of the experience to share with the class. Foster a love of healthy eating as well as family time!

Give blood. Blood is needed for many lifesaving things and can't be manufactured. One blood donation can save up to three lives! You can also help set up a drive in your community. RedCrossBlood.org has information to help plan an event.

Be aware of signs of *domestic violence* so that you can avoid it in your own life, or spot signs of someone else being in an abusive situation. Professional resources like TheHotline.org and HotPeachPages.net have information on the signs of abuse, as well as emergency contact services.

Make a field trip out of *kid art*. Have a group of kids draw, paint, sticker, or craft some art. Then, take the kids to a place like a fire station to hand deliver the adorable artwork to an audience who will be thankful for it!

See what eviction support resources are available in your area, and create a list of them to share online or with any organizations that work with *low-income* members of your community.

Share *shelter animal* pictures on social media to increase the chances of a perfect match. Pets brighten up the world!

If you work in media, check in on yourself to make sure you do not accidentally demonize groups or neighborhoods by only covering *negative news* relating to them. Try to proactively cover stories about good things the residents are doing!

Help create after-school programs that support the *social and emotional development* of kids, in addition to their academic development. Options like creative writing, theater, musical groups, business planning, STEM (science, technology, engineering, and mathematics) contests, and other creative programs help kids become well rounded and encourage them to discover new passions. Suggest ideas to your parent-teacher association, teachers, or the school board.

Create a *fan-based* charity event. If you love Star Wars, Star Trek, or any other franchise with a big fan following, create a volunteering or fundraising event where people can participate in costume.

Make memes for good. *Memes* run the gamut, but can be a fun way to use humor to gain attention for an issue. Keep them clean and inoffensive, and get creative! Share your ideas with your favorite nonprofits so they can share the memes on social media and spread the fun awareness!

Donate diverse *picture books* to nonacademic places where many kids may be, like doctors' offices, places of worship, and recreational centers.

Launch or support *entrepreneurial classes* and resources in an area where there are not currently many businesses by working with local businesses, schools, or government agencies to kick off programs. There is a lot of readily available support for entrepreneurs and small businesses online, like Clarity or SCORE (mentoring); *Udemy*, *Coursera*, or *Lynda.com* (online classes); and GAN, the Global Accelerator Network (a start-up accelerator for financing), that you can offer up in your community.

Create *family play spaces* in areas that might not typically have one, like a grocery store, church, or hospital. Playrooms allow for moms, dads, grandparents, and younger kids to spend quality time together playing. With games, books, crafts, puzzles, toys, and activities, everyone can have some fun!

Hold an activity for young kids where they can create "feelings puppets." While having fun and being artistic, kids can talk through the puppets about things that are on their mind, learning to share feelings in a healthy way.

Print your thoughts on T-shirts. You can use websites like *Custom Ink*, *UberPrints*, or *CafePress* to create a design in honor of a favorite cause. Consider giving the T-shirts to other people who will wear them to support the cause as well.

Create or support an organization that helps kids become entrepreneurs. Owning your own business is a great way to become self-sufficient, and the skills needed to create and run a small business are invaluable.

Create a phone (or texting) tree for emergencies. If something happens, have a way to connect with others in your community quickly by establishing a phone or call tree where each person is responsible for contacting a few people. Group *text messages* work as well. Keep a list handy with all of the phone numbers you need for the group, and you're all set!

Teach young kids about giving by having them select a toy of theirs to give to a *less fortunate* child. This can be a nice classroom project for kindergartners or preschoolers. Letting kids experience the joyful feeling generosity creates helps encourage a lifelong love of changing the world!

Create a *comedy troupe* at your school or local community center. Laughter is the best medicine!

Make a list of easy volunteering ideas for *kids and parents* to do together, and distribute it to local schools.

Give someone *clean water* to drink in another part of the world. Globally, one out of every nine people doesn't have access to clean water. Donating to organizations like CharityWater.org, Water.org, and Planet-Water.org helps provide clean water through activities like building wells or filtration systems. Help quench someone's thirst, safely!

Support a local *historical* place by holding an event there. Events like nonprofit galas, corporate dinners, awards ceremonies, or movie screenings can all be more interesting when held at unusual places, and it helps support the historical venue!

Make recycling bin covers or paint recycling bins in fun, artistic ways to make common spaces more beautiful, and encourage more people to recycle.

Help a youth group set up a table at a local high school to provide voting information and to help eligible kids register to vote.

Ask people to volunteer to bring friendly dogs to college campuses during finals week. Those adorable fluffy bundles of energy are just the thing to calm and relax stressed-out students!

Take a responsible *gap year*. A gap year is usually a year between high school and university and can be used for volunteering abroad or at home. If you're planning a gap year volunteering experience, research local places to travel to and learn from the local culture. This way, you can help in ways the community specifically needs.

Give kids (age-appropriate) gifts like clay, blocks, or sandboxes that have unlimited possibilities to *fuel imagination*!

Create a *mobile farmers' market*. A mobile farmers' market can supply fresh and healthy fruits and vegetables, and can be stocked by local farmers.

Become a Court Appointed *Special Advocate* for children in foster care. Within the legal systems, these are people who listen to a child and the people around them, and let judges know what the child needs. No need to be trained in legal or social services: training is provided! If this opportunity does not exist in your country, look for other volunteer roles to help children in foster care.

Host a *movie night* at your local library. Libraries are valuable public spaces that can be used for all sorts of fun and educational purposes. Sponsor a movie party at your local library where everyone can connect and maybe learn something new.

Ask local hospitals or clinics to provide *mobile healthcare* or dental care. Some people can't get to a doctor or dentist. Mobile health and dental care can help people in your community have better access to good health!

Get a group together to *go caroling* around the holidays. Spread some cheer!

Smile at a stranger, and make two people happy!

Give **good reviews** to places you think make the world better. Review hotels, restaurants, museums, stores—if you love it, write a good review online! Globally, people make decisions every day based on the opinions of others.

Help teachers get training to create trauma-informed classrooms. By being aware of the impact traumatic events and situations have on kids, teachers and administrators can be better prepared to recognize and respond to kids who have experienced trauma. **Trauma-sensitive** resources, information, and programs like MindUP, Sound Discipline, FuelEd, and MeMoves can be found at CreatingTraumaSensitiveSchools.org.

Teach kids *Internet safety tips* like turning off their location on apps, and never posting their address, email, or phone number online. The Internet can be a valuable tool as long as you stay safe!

Collect cell phones, smartphones, or tablets for soldiers or medical workers *overseas*. Programs like CellPhonesforSoldiers.com and MedicMobile.org provide shipping labels, and even broken phones are gladly accepted.

Sign kids up for *library cards* to help them develop a love of books and reading that will benefit them for life.

Have a group of people draw pretty artwork, inspiring quotes, or fun sayings with chalk on *local sidewalks*. You'll be sure to put a smile on the faces of neighbors and visitors alike.

Help create better *captions* on online videos to help those who are hard of hearing. Autogenerated captions aren't always correct, so if you leave comments with corrections on videos for the creators, they can be edited to be more precise so everyone can get the full story.

Protest *unfair punishments*. Groups like Human Rights Watch, Amnesty International, and the International Federation for Human Rights keep tabs on stories like women being sentenced to death for defending themselves against sexual assault, or protestors being sentenced to life in prison for speaking up. These organizations also offer ways for you to help protest.

Help a local school create a modern *antibullying* policy.

Create a "Positively _____" page online, either a social media page or a website. Promote all of the *positive* things happening in your city, organization, school, or neighborhood.

Make *holiday cards* that have a cause-related message, like adopting shelter pets or donating coats and gloves to kids. Inspire kindhearted actions as you send holiday wishes to friends and family.

Run a *jeans drive*. See how many pairs of jeans you can collect for those who are experiencing homelessness.

Provide livestock to a family. Heifer International focuses on teaching *sustainable farming* and giving farmers access to markets. Livestock is given to families along with training, and the families then pass on the offspring of their livestock to others. Check out Heifer.org for various ways to get involved and make donations.

Carry your *trash* around with you for one whole day. Then, talk about your experience online in a short video or post with photos. It is enlightening to see how much trash the average person creates in just one day.

Research *part-time jobs* for kids in high school and provide the list to local schools. Early experience with working creates a good work ethic that is helpful for the future.

Make kids experiencing homelessness feel like *superheroes*. Create kits with capes and masks to give to local shelters.

Get Out the Vote. GOTV campaigns help people see the reasons why voting is in their own self-interest. Especially in areas with traditionally low turnout, or in areas where the vote can swing with better turnout, getting everyone involved in their own destiny is really critical!

Ask kids how they think they can help *combat bullying*. Kids know how other kids their age see things. So ask them for their ideas, and implement any good ones in a school, playground, or community center.

Support robotics programs in your local elementary schools, especially for girls. Still far fewer women than men go into *STEM* (science, technology, engineering, and mathematics) around the world. Fun, challenging, and interesting programs like robotics can help girls, and boys, develop an interest in STEM fields by sparking curiosity. And those brilliant minds might later help create world-changing breakthroughs we can't even imagine today!

Start a *fitness club* in your neighborhood to help everyone be healthier.

Contribute to a capital campaign to build or renovate a building in your community. You can help with these "brick and mortar" campaigns by supporting fundraising events, or donating to creative options like buying a brick with your name engraved on it that is used on pathways or in the building.

Get some budding chefs together to create meals for volunteers. Is there a Habitat for Humanity house being built in your town? Support the volunteers with home-cooked lunches or dinners!

Take a group of teens from urban areas hiking or climbing. In cities, there is often not much access to the great outdoors. Help expand the horizons and worldview of local kids by arranging an activity that involves nature.

Help grant seniors' wishes. Take a page from organizations like Twilight Wish Foundation, and help a *senior citizen* get their wish during their twilight years.

Work with animals in distress through *compassionate travel*. You can volunteer to help animals at your next travel destination, and, at the same time, avoid problematic animal tourist attractions as well.

Stick a *high-profile volunteer* (a school principal, perhaps?) to a wall for a good cause. Sell pieces of duct tape, have people write why they support the cause on the tape, and stick away! It's a hilarious way to get donations and awareness for a cause that really *sticks* with you.

Remind any adults over age fifty-five to get their *blood pressure* checked regularly. Pressures of 130 over 80 or higher can mean an increased risk of stroke or heart disease, so knowing about and treating high blood pressure can quite literally save a life!

Hold a drive for *board and card games,* then donate the games to local shelters or community centers.

Hold a *dance class* at a senior center. Bring some friends to dance along, and everyone will have a ball!

Organize a trash cleanup *relay race* with local sports teams. The team that collects the most trash in the least amount of time can win a prize.

Make kitties more adoptable. Get a group together to go to a local pet shelter on a regular basis to play with the *cats and kittens*. Socializing these furry felines helps them to be more comfortable with people, making them more likely to be adopted.

Share your newfound ways to change the world with a *friend*!

ABOUT THE AUTHOR

Amy Neumann is a social good fanatic who has been working professionally to help create positive change for many years. After spending sixteen years in Los Angeles with companies like AT&T and Yahoo!, and working on national and international nonprofit projects, Amy returned to Cleveland, Ohio. A curiosity about how technology and creativity can help change the world has led Amy into interviews, conversations, research, and experiments about social good and positive change ideas. An entrepreneur by nature, Amy recently founded a startup nonprofit called Free Tech for Nonprofits to help small nonprofits do more of their important work faster. She is involved with industrious organizations and individuals daily at Case Western Reserve University's collaborative First Year Cleveland project to reduce infant mortality. Amy often speaks at events like Dell's Social Innovation Conference and ASU's Sustainability Conference. She is widely published, including as a contributor to *Forbes*, an author of PR News's *Crisis Management Guidebook*, and a columnist for *HuffPost*. Because she can't get enough of innovative world-changers, Amy also publishes under her social enterprise consultancy, Good Plus Tech, as well as her passion project, CharityIdeas.org.

Everyday Ways to Make a Difference ✋

SIMPLE ACTS TO
Save Our Planet

**500 WAYS TO
MAKE A DIFFERENCE**
MICHELLE NEFF

SIMPLE
ACTS
~ OF ~
KINDNESS
500+ Ways to Make
a Difference

adamsmedia
An Imprint of Simon & Schuster
A CBS COMPANY

DEC 1 2 2018